THE
NORTH YORKSHIRE
COOK BOOK SECOND HELPINGS

A CELEBRATION OF THE AMAZING FOOD & DRINK ON OUR DOORSTEP

The North Yorkshire Cook Book:
Second Helpings

©2019 Meze Publishing Ltd. All rights reserved.

First edition printed in 2019 in the UK.

ISBN: 9781910863565

Thank you: Tommy Banks, Roots York

Compiled by: Emma Toogood

Written by: Katie Fisher and Kate Reeves-Brown

Photography by: Tim Green
(www.timgreenphotographer.com)

Additional Photography: Matt Crowder,
Marc Barker, Shutterstock

Edited by: Phil Turner, Chris Brierley

Designed by: Phil Turner, Paul Cocker

Contributors: Ruth Alexander, Lydia Fitzsimons,
Marek Nowicki, Michael Johnson, Sarah Koriba,
Rupinder Casimir

Cover art: David Broadbent
(www.davidbroadbent.co.uk)

Printed in Great Britain by Bell and Bain Ltd, Glasgow

me:ze
PUBLISHING

Published by Meze Publishing Limited
Unit 1b, 2 Kelham Square
Kelham Riverside
Sheffield S3 8SD
Web: www.mezepublishing.co.uk
Telephone: 0114 275 7709
Email: info@mezepublishing.co.uk

FOREWORD

NORTH YORKSHIRE IS MY HOME AND I'D NEVER MOVE AWAY.

It's a wonderfully diverse county from a culinary perspective and I think the food and drink industry here is really booming at the moment. Our very rural environment provides opportunities to do something different and meet the challenge of using all the amazing produce grown and reared across the region.

Our livestock and grazing is some of the best in the whole country, plus it's the game capital of the UK and we have coastline as well – the fact that loads of North Yorkshire's produce is used in the top London restaurants says it all really. That struck me straight away when I first did work experience down there, because it seemed mad that we were working with stuff grown five miles from my home.

We also have so much going for us from a leisure perspective. Every village has a pub, every town has several – you only have to go a couple of miles to find another! It's a great part of North Yorkshire culture that goes hand in hand with the county's great beer. I love finding a good pub to sit and eat in where the food is simple but done really well.

I'm lucky to have insider knowledge, but if you're a visitor then it might be hard to know where to start. This book is a great opportunity for some of the best places to get exposure, especially if they're smaller and maybe not so well known, and a way to celebrate all the good things that they do.

It's still so exciting for me to see how much the whole scene is improving here – three restaurants in York were listed in the worldwide top 100 for 2019, which is the first time any restaurant in York has made the list. There's never been a better time to cook, visit, eat and drink in North Yorkshire.

Tommy Banks

CONTENTS

FOREWORD

Tommy Banks, Roots York — 6

ASHLEY MCCARTHY CHOCOLATE

Raising the bar — 10
Chocolate florentines — 12

BEADLAM GRANGE FARM SHOP

From the heart of Yorkshire — 14
Blue cheese steak burger — 16

THE BISHY WEIGH

Shop for change — 18
Minestrone and homemade bread — 20
Mushroom risotto with roast butternut squash — 22
Sticky toffee crumble cake with custard — 24

CRUMBS CUPCAKERY

Have your cake and eat it — 26
Chocolate orange cupcakes — 28

EAT ME CAFÉ

Scarborough fare — 30
Lamb meatballs with endive, shallots and borlotti beans — 32
Seared steak and egg donburi — 34

EVIL EYE

Step into the weird and wonderful — 36
Bitter ex — 38
Napoleon dynamite — 40
Two martinis — 42

THE CAFÉ AT FIELD AND FAWCETT

Wined and dined — 44
Country pork terrine with cornichons and toasted
sourdough bread — 46
Food & drink pairings — 48

THE GRANTLEY BAR & RESTAURANT

Relaxed elegance — 54
Grantley bread and butter pudding — 56

GRANTLEY HALL

The best of both worlds — 58
Restaurant eightyeight's grilled mackerel kabayaki — 60
Shaun Rankin's lamb with jerusalem artichoke
and ribblesdale cheese — 62
Fletchers Restaurant's braised Waterford
farm beef cheek — 64

HAXBY BAKEHOUSE

Real bread — 66
The Yorkshire 85 sourdough — 68

JERVAULX ABBEY TEAROOM

Life is what you bake it — 70
Free-from raspberry and almond cake — 72
Wensleydale, ginger and apricot cheesecake — 74
Carrot and coconut cake — 76

LOVE CHEESE

For the love of cheese — 78

THE WHIPPET INN

A taste of Yorkshire — 80
Love Cheese & The Whippet Inn's beef rib curry and
Yorkshire halloumi saag paneer — 82

NORTHERN FOX YORKSHIRE GINS

Craft gins of Yorkshire — 90
Little Wold honeyberry fizz — 92
Dry classic gin & tonic — 94
Traditional pink gin crush — 96
Liquorice espresso martini — 98

THE PIEBALD INN

Far from a one trick pony — 100
The Yorkshire coach horse pie — 102

THE PLOUGH INN

Dinner and a show — 104
Ale braised beef short rib, spelt and sage pesto — 106

ROOTS YORK

Getting back to our roots   108
Oats, berries and tarragon   110

SKOSH

Fusion flavours   112
Pork belly 'massaman' with apple and peanut   114

SPIRIT OF YORKSHIRE DISTILLERY

Whisky business   116
Filey bay espresso martini and macarons   118

VALE OF MOWBRAY

Yorkshire baked and brewed   120
Sweet chilli garlic sauce with zesty onions   122

VISIT YORK

The city with taste   124
Immersive culinary experiences   126

WENSLEYDALE CREAMERY

Iconic Yorkshire Wensleydale   128
Pizza with parma ham, avocado and Yorkshire
Wensleydale cheese   130

WHERE THE RIBBON ENDS

A perfect match   132
Bespoke cookies   134
Brownie stacks   136
Classic vanilla cupcakes with buttercream   138

THE WHOLE HOGG FARM SHOP

Tastes like home   140
Pumpkin soup   142

YORK GIN

Distilling tradition   144
York Gin classic cocktails   146

THE YORK ROAST CO

Lunch all wrapped up!   148
War of the Roses   150

RAISING THE BAR

ASHLEY MCCARTHY IS A SELF-TAUGHT CHOCOLATIER, AS WELL AS RUNNING YE OLD SUN INN IN COLTON WITH HIS WIFE KELLY.

Ashley's chocolate business has humble beginnings. Wanting quality in every aspect at Ye Old Sun Inn, the pub he runs with his wife Kelly, but lacking a pastry chef, he started to dabble in chocolate making. He's a chef at heart, not a trained chocolatier, but soon began to discover a new passion. He started out making petit fours and designated part of the pub as a small shop area to sell handmade chocolates over Christmas. It wasn't long before customers started requesting commissions such as personalised wedding favours.

"That's the fun side," says Ashley. He was, for example, recently commissioned to make an almost life-size chocolate Elvis which stood at a staggering five feet tall! The visuals are an incredibly important aspect of these chocolatey sculptures, always ornate and unique to the customer. And the fun doesn't stop there. Recently, Ashley and Kelly have started experimenting with gin-infused chocolate. They currently use York Gin, and aim to support other local suppliers wherever possible.

There are four varieties of gin-infused chocolates which have proved to be best sellers and even won a Taste Award from Deliciouslyorkshire. They have big plans for the future, too, as Kelly aims to start distilling her own gin soon. The enterprising couple are always looking to refine the process, trialling traditional and eclectic flavours to develop their own style.

Ashley is widely known, not least for his involvement in Channel Four's show 'Extreme Chocolate Makers' but for the work he does in the community too. He makes a chocolate sculpture every year which stays in the pub to collect charity donations, which are taken to the Martin House hospice on Christmas Eve.

If that wasn't enough, Ashley attends local food festivals where he does demonstrations with his son Ben. He also leads chocolate making workshops at the pub for smaller groups. Looking to the future, he wants to move things in his own direction, with plans to operate the workshops from a purpose-built cookery school soon and continue building his chocolate business.

CHOCOLATE FLORENTINES

I've chosen this classic recipe as it has been in my family for many years. Handed down from my mother from her mother, I'm sure it's been tweaked over the years to accommodate new tastes and fashion but they are always a firm favourite, especially at Christmas. These little delicate chocolates offer everything that makes you think of Christmas, decadence and luxury... all in one bite.

25g butter

75g golden caster sugar

10g plain flour

65ml double cream

50g whole pistachios, cut into thin slivers

50g ready-flaked almonds

50g whole candied peel, chopped

25g glacé cherries, chopped

25g sultanas

175g dark chocolate (minimum 70% cocoa solids)

Start by melting the butter with the sugar in a small, heavy-based saucepan over a very low heat. Add the flour and keep stirring until the mixture has come together.

Gradually add the cream, stirring continuously to keep it smooth. Then add all the remaining ingredients, except the chocolate. Stir thoroughly again, then remove the saucepan from the heat and put the mixture to one side to cool.

You'll find it easier to bake one sheet of the florentines at a time, so line two or three flat trays with baking paper then place heaped teaspoonfuls of the mixture onto one of the prepared baking sheets, spacing them about 2½cm apart to allow the mixture room to expand while baking.

Flatten each spoonful with the back of the spoon, then bake on the top shelf of a preheated oven at 190°c for about 10 to 12 minutes, or until golden. Take the florentines out of the oven and leave them to harden on the baking sheet for 2 to 3 minutes before quickly transferring them to a wire rack to cool completely. Repeat in batches until the mixture is all used.

Melt the dark chocolate in a bowl over a saucepan of simmering water, making sure the base of the bowl doesn't touch the water.

Place the cooled florentines bottom up on the wire rack and, using a teaspoon, coat the underside of each one with warm melted chocolate. Just before it sets, make a pattern of wavy lines on each one, using a fork. Now leave the florentines to cool completely again so the chocolate sets hard before packing them (alternating rows of fruit and chocolate side up) in airtight tins.

Preparation time: 10 minutes | Cooking time: 20-30 minutes | Makes about 20

FROM THE
HEART OF YORKSHIRE

SET ON 300 ACRES OF MIXED FARMLAND, BEADLAM GRANGE FARM SHOP AND TEAROOM MAKES THE MOST OF ITS BEAUTIFUL SETTING AND HOMEGROWN PRODUCE.

In 2007 Mark and Jenny Rooke welcomed their first customers into Beadlam Grange Farm Shop and Tearoom. Their aim was to supply the local community with top-quality produce from their own farm and from other Yorkshire producers.

Over a decade later and the farm, with its 100 Limousin suckler cows, remains at the heart of the business. Father and son Mark and Peter breed and rear the cattle to the highest animal welfare standards, allowing full traceability for the farm shop's customers – who buy their beef metres away from the fields in which the home-bred cattle are reared. The beef is the focus of the onsite butchery (which also prepares and sells local lamb, pork, chicken and game) and symbolises what makes the farm so unique – the beef is reared on the farm, sold on the farm and transformed into delicious meals in the tearoom. The Sunday lunch is a must!

The mouth-watering delicatessen boasts a large selection of cheeses from Yorkshire producers, as well as home-cooked meats, local pork pies and delicious desserts. The shop sells all the essentials from local suppliers – bread, milk, vegetables, preserves, biscuits and cakes, oils and dressings, and gins and liqueurs to name but a few... The team of staff, who share the family's commitment to quality, contribute to the friendly atmosphere, chatting to regulars and getting to know new faces.

The tearoom is known for its fresh homemade sandwiches, salads and of course those home-baked cakes and treats. The farmhouse breakfasts are made fresh to order, as are the lunches and afternoon teas. The Sunday roasts are understandably popular, so booking is advisable. They have the advantage of being fully licensed, offering an excellent selection of wines and beers to accompany your meal.

They aim to be as accommodating as possible. Dogs are welcome on the picnic tables in the covered barn, and there are tables next to the children's play area for parents with younger children. They also have a couple of tables in the farm shop with waitress service for those unable to use the stairs.

They are continually striving to maintain their excellent reputation thanks to their farm-to-fork philosophy and commitment to excellence. And with the next generation (Peter's son William) keen to get stuck in, they are as excited about the future as they are proud of their heritage.

BLUE CHEESE STEAK BURGER

Ask for coarse minced flank from your butcher to make our steak burger. This has a larger fat content than standard burger mixes, which adds to the flavour, and most of the fat will render out while cooking.

200g beef flank, coarsely minced

1 slice of Shepherd's Purse Yorkshire Blue Cheese

1 tsp mayonnaise

1 tsp English mustard

1 tsp tomato ketchup

1 burger bun

1 iceberg lettuce leaf, shredded

1 slice of beef tomato

Salt and pepper

Gently squeeze the minced beef together with cupped hands, then gently press the ball into an even patty.

Place the burger patty between two sheets of baking parchment and refrigerate for at least an hour.

When ready to cook, heat a heavy-bottomed pan on a medium-high heat. Remove the burger patties from the fridge and season with salt and pepper on both sides.

Fry the patties until cooked through and still juicy. Before the end of cooking, add one thin slice of Yorkshire Blue Cheese and allow to melt.

To make the burger sauce, mix the mayonnaise, mustard and tomato ketchup together.

Slice the bread bun in half and toast either under the grill or in a dry frying pan for 1 minute. Assemble the burger on the toasted bread bun with the lettuce, tomato and burger sauce.

Preparation time: 10 minutes | Cooking time: 10 minutes | Serves 1

SHOP FOR CHANGE

THE BISHY WEIGH IS A PLASTIC-FREE SHOP ON BISHOPTHORPE ROAD IN YORK, ENCOURAGING REDUCED-WASTE SHOPPING FOR ALL YOUR FOOD AND HOUSEHOLD NEEDS.

The key idea behind York's independent eco-friendly shop, The Bishy Weigh, is to make little green lifestyle changes more accessible and an easy part of everyday life. Owner Alice has drawn on first-hand experience to set the plastic-free venture up; she started to look at the impact of plastic pollution more seriously in 2018 – along with plenty of others, during what has been dubbed 'the Blue Planet II effect' – and realised that food packaging was a real obstacle to living more sustainably.

The Bishy Weigh is her local solution to this problem, and has quickly found a niche in the community on Bishopthorpe Road. The Bishy Weigh aims to cover as many bases as possible. Among the hundreds of products you can refill your containers or the shop's paper bags with, you will find ingredients for baking and cooking, environmentally-friendly cleaning products, toiletries and self-care products, and containers to buy the products in like glass jars and tins.

The shop's 'weigh and pay' system also welcomes resourcefulness when it comes to bringing your own containers…the team have come across all sorts! Everyone who is employed at The Bishy Weigh is dedicated to the ethos behind the business, helping people to shop and live more sustainably day-to-day in ways that do make a positive impact.

Alice knows that living in a more sustainable way isn't just about what we buy, and so collaborates with other local organisations to put on events such as clothes swaps, repairing and upcycling workshops, and to share information about community gardening and composting, how to recycle more effectively and how to reduce food waste, to give people the confidence and tools to tackle the problem of plastics.

Sir David Attenborough may be the figurehead of 'the Blue Planet II effect' which inspired Alice to open The Bishy Weigh, but she also credits him for the inspiration behind her bakery business, White Rose Bakes. She used to work in TV production and was asked to make a birthday cake for the man himself while working on a programme of his! Some of her delicious bakes are sold in The Bishy Weigh, from vegan-friendly slices to their infamous sea-salted caramel millionaire's shortbread. So you can feed yourself well while doing good for the planet – what's not to love?

MINESTRONE AND HOMEMADE BREAD

Coming from a family of foodies, this is my version of one of my childhood favourites: 'minestrone like mama used to make', served with my 'fake it 'til you make it' bread. Artisan sourdough this is not. However, it can still make your dreams come true…if you dream of wowing your family and friends with delicious homemade bread, with no packaging or preservatives and very little hands-on time or skill needed.

FOR THE BREAD

450g strong white bread flour

½ tsp quick yeast

1¾ tsp fine sea salt

375ml warm water

4 tbsp semolina

FOR THE SOUP

1 tbsp rapeseed oil

1 small onion, finely chopped

2 sticks of celery, chopped into small pieces

1 red pepper, chopped into small pieces

1 tsp garlic flakes

2 litres vegetable stock

1 400g tin chopped tomatoes

8 sun-dried tomatoes, finely chopped

1 bay leaf

½ tsp dried oregano

1 tsp dried basil

¼ tsp dried rosemary

60g chiferetti or macaroni

200g cooked cannellini beans

1 tbsp soy sauce

1 tsp salt

Cracked black pepper, to taste

Parmesan, grated (optional)

Mix the flour, yeast and salt together in a bowl. Add the water and stir until fully combined. That's it! Cover the bowl and leave the dough to prove at room temperature for 12 hours.

After 12 hours, place a lidded cast iron casserole dish in the oven (one that is 18cm in diameter is ideal to get the best boule-shaped loaf) and preheat to 230°c for 15 to 20 minutes.

Carefully lift the hot pot out of the oven and sprinkle three tablespoons of the semolina over the base. This prevents the bread from sticking. Pour in the proved bread dough, sprinkle the remaining semolina on top, and replace the lid. Bake for 30 minutes with the lid on, then a further 10 minutes without the lid, or until the loaf is golden brown. When done, tip the loaf out of the pot to cool on a wire rack. You may need to run a knife around the edge to loosen it first.

Make the soup while the bread is baking and cooling. Heat the oil in a large saucepan, then gently fry the onion, celery, red pepper and garlic in a large saucepan to soften for approximately 10 minutes. Add the stock, tomatoes, herbs, pasta, beans, soy sauce and seasoning. Bring to the boil and simmer for 20 minutes with the lid slightly ajar.

Ladle the minestrone into bowls and top with a little heap of grated Parmesan if you wish. Serve immediately with your delicious homemade bread!

Notes: This basic loaf is great to serve with soup, or for making sandwiches and toast. But you can also get creative with it: why not add a couple of tablespoons of sunflower seeds and pumpkin seeds, or a handful of chopped dried fruits and a teaspoon of cinnamon? You can also play with different flours, swapping out some of the white bread flour for wholemeal, spelt or rye.

Preparation time: 10 minutes, plus 12 hours proving | Cooking time: 1 hour 10 minutes | Serves: 4-6

MUSHROOM RISOTTO WITH ROAST BUTTERNUT SQUASH

This recipe represents just one of many delicious meals that can be made entirely without packaging or waste!

10g dried forest mushrooms

1 large butternut squash

3 tbsp Yorkshire rapeseed oil

1 tbsp nutritional yeast

1 tsp chilli flakes

Salt and black pepper

2 shallots, finely chopped

200g chestnut mushrooms, washed and quartered

2 tbsp pumpkin seeds

1 tsp garlic flakes

300g Arborio rice

150ml white wine (or 150ml additional stock if preferred)

1/3 tsp dried rosemary

2/3 tsp dried thyme

Preheat the oven to 200°c.

Soak the dried mushrooms in a litre of boiled water (or 1150ml if you are omitting the wine). Set aside for 30 minutes, while you continue to prepare the other elements.

Remove the skin and seeds from the butternut squash and cut into chunks 1cm thick. Lay out in a single layer on a baking tray. Drizzle with two tablespoons of the Yorkshire rapeseed oil, sprinkle with the nutritional yeast, chilli flakes, and a little salt and pepper then toss to evenly coat the squash pieces. Roast in the preheated oven for 45 minutes.

While the squash is roasting, wash and chop the shallots and chestnut mushrooms.

Heat a dry pan on a medium-low heat. Add the pumpkin seeds and toss until lightly toasted, then set aside for later. Add a tablespoon of Yorkshire rapeseed oil to the same pan. Continuing on a medium to low heat, gently fry the shallots and garlic flakes to soften.

Add the rice and toss for a minute or two to coat the rice in the oil. Then add the white wine (or 150ml of the mushroom stock if omitting the wine). When the wine has been absorbed by the rice, add the herbs, soaked mushrooms, and 200ml of the mushroom stock. Each time the stock cooks into the rice, add another 200ml. Add the chestnut mushrooms and seasoning with the last part of the stock. The whole process should take 20 to 25 minutes.

TO SERVE

Top a pile of risotto with butternut squash pieces and a sprinkle of the toasted pumpkin seeds.

Preparation time: 20 minutes | Cooking time: 45 minutes | Serves: 4

STICKY TOFFEE CRUMBLE CAKE WITH CUSTARD

Because why have one winter favourite when you can have two?

FOR THE DATE PASTE

150g dates, chopped
170ml water

FOR THE CRUMBLE TOPPING

85g Demerara sugar
85g salted butter
85g self-raising flour
30g jumbo oats
15ml milk
1 tsp vanilla bean paste

FOR THE CAKE

2 medium pears (approximately 200g)
200g blackberries
100g salted butter, melted
100g light brown sugar
40g golden syrup
1 tsp vanilla bean paste
2 large free-range eggs
225g self-raising flour
1 tsp cinnamon
½ tsp ground cardamom
½ tsp bicarbonate of soda

FOR THE CUSTARD

800ml milk
40g caster sugar
4 large free-range egg yolks
4 tsp cornflour
2 tsp vanilla bean paste

Preheat the oven to 180°c and line a 20cm square, deep cake pan with baking paper.

Add the dates and water to a saucepan and cook on a low heat while stirring (ideally with a silicone spatula) for around 5 minutes until it forms a thick, smooth paste. Set this aside to cool down while you prepare the crumble topping.

Put all the crumble ingredients into a bowl and rub together until combined. Set aside in the fridge.

Wash, peel, quarter, core and finely slice the pears. Wash and drain the blackberries.

For the cake batter, add the date paste, melted butter, sugar, syrup and vanilla to a bowl and mix together. Add the eggs and mix again. Sift in the flour, spices and bicarbonate of soda. Gently fold together until just combined and pour into the prepared cake pan.

Lay the pear slices over the cake batter in an even layer, and the blackberries evenly on top of the pears. Sprinkle the crumble over the fruit and bake for 60 minutes.

To prepare the custard, add the milk to a saucepan, bring to the boil, then remove from the heat. In a separate bowl, whisk together the sugar, egg yolks, cornflour and vanilla until smooth. While continuing to whisk, gradually add the hot milk to the egg mixture until fully combined. Pour the custard back into the pan and cook on a low heat while stirring until thickened enough to coat the back of the spatula. This should take 15 to 20 minutes.

Serve up the warm cake with a generous drizzle of the fresh custard.

Preparation time: 20 minutes | Cooking time: 80 minutes | Serves: 12 (with 4 portions of custard)

HAVE YOUR CAKE

AND EAT IT

RUN BY TWO SISTERS AND A SMALL FRIENDLY TEAM, CRUMBS CUPCAKERY IS ALL ABOUT GREAT CAKE IN A GREAT ATMOSPHERE AT THE SHOP AND CAFÉ IN YORK.

Crumbs Cupcakery is owned by twin sisters Charlotte and Jennifer Davison, who took on the business in January 2018 at the age of 20. They decided to take the plunge because both wanted to create an environment that was fun for staff and customers: what better way to do so than with cake? Crumbs has a small and extremely tight-knit team of bakers – Alex Timotheou and Mikhail Lim – and waitressing staff, led by the twins who both bake and work in the shop every day of the week between them. They serve a variety of sweet treats, with a wide range of cupcakes as the star attraction. Chocolate Brownie and Caramel Fudge cupcakes are firm favourites!

Everything is made on site to make sure customers get the freshest cakes possible. The menu includes a daily changing special which is up to the baker on the day, encouraging creativity. The other nine cupcakes include a mixture of classics and some more unusual flavours, alongside gluten-free cupcakes and vegan cupcakes on request. The commitment to baking all their products on site daily has ensured that Crumbs really stands out, even being named one of the city's top four Cafés of the Year by Visit York in 2019.

The café, bakery and shop is housed in a beautiful old building which is owned by the nearby York Minster. The outdoor tables overlook this architectural gem, and the café caters for young and old to enjoy the view with afternoon tea, cream tea and a large drinks menu available. The Victoria 99 – a cupcake topped with sprinkles and a flake to look like an ice cream – is always a hit with children. Charlotte and Jen pride themselves on the customer service, creating a friendly environment that keeps customers new and old coming to see them.

Crumbs Cupcakery also caters for those special occasions when only the best cake will do; the team enjoy being part of weddings and birthdays by providing extra large cupcakes, personalised bakes, cupcake towers and large celebration cakes for everyone to indulge in. The team also regularly head off to food shows around the country, and offer cupcake decorating parties for kids and big kids alike at the bakery. The young owners hope to expand their business in future by bringing sweet treats to more of the UK, because who doesn't love a cupcake!

Welcome LoVeLy YoU

Crumbs
CUPCAKERY
01904 638282

CAKE
IS
FOR LIFE
NOT
JUST FOR
BIRTHDAYS

CHOCOLATE ORANGE CUPCAKES

Being from York – the original home of Terry's – who doesn't love chocolate oranges! We find this cupcake is brilliant to serve all year round but becomes a firm favourite around Christmas time.

FOR THE CUPCAKES

280g caster sugar

200g plain flour

40g cocoa powder

1 tbsp baking powder

200ml milk

2 eggs

1 orange, zested

80g baking margarine (we use Stork)

1 Terry's Chocolate Orange

FOR THE ICING

300g unsalted butter

385g icing sugar

½ tsp orange essence

50g milk or dark chocolate, melted

Weigh all the dry ingredients into a bowl and mix everything together. Measure the milk in a jug, crack in the eggs and add the orange zest then whisk everything together. Add the baking margarine to the bowl with the dry ingredients, then slowly pour the egg and milk mixture in while beating with an electric mixer. Continue until the batter is smooth and free from lumps.

Set out paper cases in a cupcake tray, then fill them half way up with cake mixture. Pop the tray in the oven and bake the cupcakes for around 10 minutes at 150°c.

In the meantime, prepare the icing. Weigh the butter in a bowl, then beat with an electric mixer until it turns pale in colour. With the mixer running slowly, gradually add the icing sugar and beat with the butter until the icing has a light texture. Now add the orange essence and melted chocolate. Mix well so the chocolate orange flavour is evenly distributed.

Once they have baked, let the cupcakes cool on a wire rack before icing with your chocolate orange buttercream using a piping bag. Top each cupcake with a chocolate orange segment and you are all done!

Preparation time: 30 minutes | Cooking time: 10-15 minutes | Makes 12 cupcakes

SCARBOROUGH FARE

COMBINING HOMELY FAVOURITES WITH WORLDLY DELIGHTS IS THE ORDER OF THE DAY AT EAT ME CAFÉ IN SCARBOROUGH, WHERE YOU WON'T FIND A DULL DISH ON THE MENU.

At Eat Me Café, owners Martyn and Stephen like to do things differently. Situated behind the famous Stephen Joseph Theatre, loyal locals and visiting sightseers can enjoy a taste of international cuisine in one of Scarborough's hidden gems, as it's been named by the Waitrose Good Food Guide for six consecutive years.

It all began in 2009, when Martyn and Stephen sought to bring together their shared passion for good food, good company and a suitably quirky venue in which to enjoy the two. The first big question was the name, Hanover Road Café or Eat Me? They went for a drive, searching for inspiration, and decided to run the two options by two elderly ladies passing by. They preferred Eat Me and so it was settled!

The saying goes that you eat with your eyes, so Martyn and Stephen have made sure that when you look at their food it really calls out 'eat me'. The menu offers a whole host of interesting options, seamlessly mixing global and local. From their time spent travelling and their aim of always putting a twist on a classic dish, what emerges is an eclectic menu. While some of their more exotic dishes require ingredients fetched from further afield, Martyn and Stephen are passionate about sourcing produce locally and supporting fellow local businesses. From Vietnamese pho and Japanese ramen to handcrafted burgers with house slaw, this is a menu with something for everyone.

The same ethos extends to the range of drinks designed to accompany any dish in the café. Eat Me boasts its own speciality coffee blends (which you won't find anywhere else) and an all-day cocktail menu. Stephen's Scottish roots are apparent when you take a look at the extensive gin selection, which includes two options from Edinburgh and three from the Shetlands, again fusing the local and homegrown with things from further flung places.

It's not just the food and drink that sets this café apart though. The vision was always for Eat Me to be a community café, not just for the tourists that flock to Scarborough over summer, but for the year-round locals "who deserve good food in a relaxed venue" as Martyn and Stephen put it. A sociable atmosphere is also important; if you arrive when there's a rush, you're encouraged to join an occupied table and get chatting! With retro inspired décor and an open-minded approach to café fare, Eat Me Café is Scarborough's quirkiest spot for foodies.

LAMB MEATBALLS WITH ENDIVE, SHALLOTS AND BORLOTTI BEANS

The last b in our burgers, bowls and balls is this luscious lamb and bean extravaganza, best served with buttered lumpy mash.

FOR THE BEANS

500g dried borlotti beans, or 2 tins

2 tsp salt

1 bay leaf

250g smoky slab bacon (optional)

FOR THE MEATBALLS

900g minced lamb

3 tbsp dried mixed herbs

1 tbsp dried rosemary

1 medium white onion, grated

1 medium clove of garlic, grated

4 large eggs, lightly beaten

200-250g fresh breadcrumbs or finely ground panko breadcrumbs

2 tsp coarse salt

½ tsp freshly ground black pepper

4 tbsp olive oil

1 litre beef or lamb stock

FOR THE VEGETABLES

60ml extra-virgin olive oil

15 large shallots, peeled and quartered

Coarse salt and freshly ground black pepper

1 head of endive (about 200g)

TO SERVE

Freshly grated Parmigiano-Reggiano cheese

Bunch of fresh flat leaf parsley

Handful of celery leaves

If using dried beans, soak them overnight in enough room temperature water to cover. The next day, drain the dried or tinned beans and place them in a saucepan with about 1.2 litres of water along with the salt, bay leaf, and bacon (if using). Simmer over a low heat for 1 to 2 hours, or until the centre of the beans have a creamy texture.

Meanwhile, prepare the meatballs by combining the lamb, mixed herbs, rosemary, onion, garlic, eggs, breadcrumbs, salt, and pepper in a large bowl. Mix with clean hands until well combined. Heat half of the olive oil in a large frying pan over medium heat. Form one small meatball and sauté until the meat is no longer pink, which should take 4 to 5 minutes. Taste the meatball and adjust the seasoning of the meat mixture as needed, such as adding more salt.

Use an ice cream scoop to form 24 evenly-sized meatballs and lay them on a rimmed baking sheet. Alternatively, divide the mixture into four and make six meatballs from each part.

Add the remaining olive oil to the pan and heat until hot but not smoking. Working in batches, brown the meatballs on all sides, allowing 5 to 6 minutes per batch. Drain the fat from the pot, then return the meatballs to the pan. Add enough beef or lamb stock to cover them. Bring the liquid to a simmer over a medium heat, then reduce the heat to low and allow the meatballs to cook gently until they are cooked through.

Remove the meatballs from the braising liquid with a slotted spoon and transfer to a large platter or baking sheet. Tent the platter with foil to keep the meatballs warm. Strain the braising liquid and reserve.

For the vegetables, heat a large sauté pan over a medium heat and add the olive oil. Add the shallots, season with salt and pepper, then cook for about 10 minutes while stirring occasionally until golden. To prepare the endive, trim the end, separate the leaves and cut each into 5cm pieces then rinse well. Add the endive to the pan, season again and cook for 2 or 3 minutes until just wilted. Add the cooked borlotti beans and about 60ml of the reserved braising liquid, stirring to combine.

TO SERVE

Spoon the vegetable and bean mixture into bowls with some of the pan juices. Top each with three or four meatballs then garnish with Parmigiano-Reggiano, fresh parsley and celery leaves.

Preparation time: 15 minutes, plus overnight if soaking dried beans | Cooking time: 1-2 hours | Serves: 6-8 (makes 24 meatballs)

SEARED STEAK AND EGG DONBURI# SEARED STEAK AND EGG DONBURI

This sweet and tangy rice bowl is the perfect comfort food for those darker evenings, when a little spicy kick is needed.

FOR THE MARINATED STEAK

120ml mirin

2 tbsp soy sauce

1 ½ tsp toasted sesame oil

1 ½ tsp rice wine vinegar

2 tbsp light brown sugar

2 tbsp finely grated Granny Smith apple

1 ½ tbsp finely chopped spring onion - white and light green parts

1 tbsp peeled and grated fresh ginger

2 cloves of garlic, grated

1 tbsp Korean gochujang chilli paste

4 200g pieces of skirt steak

FOR THE KIMCHI RICE

250g sushi rice

Pinch of coarse salt

2 tbsp plus 1 tsp vegetable oil

200g kimchi, coarsely chopped

2 tbsp unseasoned rice wine vinegar

Freshly ground black pepper

4 large eggs

20g baby rocket

1 tbsp extra-virgin olive oil

Chopped spring onions, to garnish

Whisk all the marinade ingredients in a large bowl. Add the steaks, then cover and chill overnight or for at least 4 hours.

To make the rice, bring about 500ml of water to the boil in a small saucepan. Add the rice and salt then bring it back to the boil. Reduce the heat to low, cover, and cook for about 20 minutes until the water has been absorbed.

Meanwhile, heat a ridged grill pan until hot. Grill the marinated steaks for about 3 minutes per side until they are slightly charred but still pink in the centre. Transfer to a plate and rest for about 5 minutes.

Heat the two tablespoons of vegetable oil in a large pan, then add the kimchi and rice wine vinegar. Stir until heated. Fold in the rice. Season the mixture to taste with salt and pepper then keep warm.

Heat the remaining teaspoon of vegetable oil in a large non-stick pan. Crack the eggs into the pan, being careful not to break the yolks. Sprinkle with salt and pepper then fry for about 3 minutes until the whites are set, and the edges become crispy.

In a small bowl, toss the baby rocket with the olive oil and season with salt and pepper.

TO SERVE

Divide the kimchi rice between four plates. Slice the steaks across the grain and arrange over the rice. Top each plate with a fried egg, scatter over the chopped spring onion, and serve with the dressed rocket. Sprinkle some toasted sesame seeds over to finish if you like, then eat!

Preparation time: 15 minutes, plus 4 hours marinating | Cooking time: 25 minutes | Serves: 4

STEP INTO THE
WEIRD AND WONDERFUL

OFFERING SANCTUARY FROM THE PLETHORA OF BUSY TOURIST ATTRACTIONS IN YORK, STEPPING INTO THE EVIL EYE TAKES YOU INTO A COLOURFUL WORLD OF MYSTICISM, WONDER AND TRAVEL...

Hidden behind a Guinness World Record-holding specialist gin shop, you'll find a colourful cocktail bar, with an equally colourful beer garden. While you can take in the view of York's iconic Minster, the atmosphere and décor will whisk you away to the vibrant bars of Brazil, Haiti and Morocco.

They sell four of their own gins: Evil SG, Evil SL, Mother of all Evil and Father of all Evil. Evil SG, created by owner Shelley Green, was inspired by childhood memories of her mum returning from Copenhagen laden down with salty Danish liquorice – a flavour that comes through in the gin. Evil SL was inspired by the flavours of Italy – think basil, oregano, orange peel, sun-dried tomatoes and rosemary – and brought to life by Sicilian-born bartender Stefano. Mother of all Evil was created by Shelley's mother and is a classic gin, similar to a London Dry, but with a bit of a kick. And finally, Father of all Evil, created by Shelley's step-father, is a flavour-packed gin they like to call, 'the zest de la zest'.

Once through the gin shop you can sip on classic cocktails or try the more adventurous concoctions that have been created by their own bartenders. If cocktails aren't your thing, there is a large selection of both local and well known ales, craft beers and ciders, alongside an epic range of spirits and mixers. There's something to please even the pickiest of palates.

Drink in hand, you're free to explore what else this 18th century building has to offer. On the first floor to the left you'll find two large, hand-carved wooden beds, perfect for lounging in. In the same room are three Stonegate facing booths, which are perfect for dreaming the world away whilst sipping on a delicious flavoured tea... or something stronger, if you prefer. On the first floor to the right is a ceiling covered in lights of all shapes and sizes – look up and let them mesmerize you while you relax in one of the Moroccan-style comfy booths. Going to the second floor, you can gaze up at the stars in this snug-style room which was purpose-built for the more social of humanity.

The term 'Evil Eye' originates in Turkey and is a symbol believed to ward off evil spirits. Here, the Evil Eye protects you from the glare of the famous Stonegate Devil who gazes right at their door. Be sure to pay both him and them a visit!

BITTER EX

Using our own Evil SG Gin, the cocktail marries flavours of liquorice with bitter yet refreshing grapefruit for a fruity, summery drink. The smoking cinnamon stick gives the drink an incredibly aromatic aroma which makes this an experience for all the senses.

¾ shot (18.75ml) lime juice

¾ shot (18.75ml) Monin Gomme

3 dashes (1ml) The Bitter Truth Bittermans Grapefruit

1 ½ shots (37.5ml) Evil gin SG

¾ shot (18.75ml) Chartreuse Green

1 shot (25ml) grapefruit juice

Ice, to serve

Grapefruit slice, to garnish

Cinnamon stick, smoking, to garnish

Stir all the ingredients together in a rocks glass with ice. Garnish with a slice of grapefruit and a smoking cinnamon stick.

Preparation time: 5 minutes each | Serves 1

NAPOLEON DYNAMITE

Our zesty Father of all Evil gin pairs a secret recipe of botanicals with the sweetness of Mandarin Napoleon and the bitterness of Campari.

Pinch of crushed black peppercorns

1 orange wedge

1 sprig of rosemary

½ shot (12.5ml) Mandarin Napoleon

1 shot (25ml) Campari

1 shot (25ml) Father of all Evil gin

Crushed ice

Soda water, to top up

1 sprig of rosemary, to garnish

Muddle the peppercorns, orange wedge and rosemary in a cocktail shaker. Add the Mandarin Napoleon, Campari and Father of all Evil Gin, and shake well. Strain onto crushed ice in a hurricane glass and top up with soda water. Garnish with a sprig of rosemary.

Preparation time: 5 minutes each | Serves 1

TWO MARTINIS

These fruity takes on a martini feature our Evil SL and Mother of all Evil gins.
Sweet and sharp flavours mingle with fresh basil and blueberries respectively.
Perfect on a warm day.

FOR THE MOJO

4 lime wedges

4 basil leaves

1 sprig of rosemary

1 shot (25ml) Monin Gomme

1 shot (25ml) Agwa

1 ½ shots (37.5ml) Evil gin SL

2 dashes (1ml) Angostura Orange Bitters

Apple juice, to top up

Basil, to garnish

FOR THE MOTHER'S RUIN

1 sprig of rosemary

Handful of blueberries

½ shot (12.5ml) lemon juice

¾ shot (18.75ml) Monin Blueberry

1 egg white

1 shot (25ml) Mother of all Evil gin

1 shot (25ml) Cointreau Blood Orange

½ shot (12.5ml) Cartron Crème de Cassis

2 dashes (1ml) The Bitter Truth
Bittermans Grapefruit

FOR THE MOJO

Muddle the lime wedges, basil and rosemary in a cocktail shaker. Add the Monin Gomme, Agwa, Evil Gin SL and Angostura Orange Bitters. Shake and fine-strain into a martini glass, then top up with apple juice. Garnish with basil.

FOR THE MOTHER'S RUIN

Shake all the ingredients in a cocktail shaker without ice, then add a generous amount of ice and shake again. Strain into a martini glass to serve.

Preparation time: 5 minutes each | Each serves 1

WINED AND DINED

GOOD WINE AND GOOD FOOD TRULY FIND THEIR MATCH MADE IN HEAVEN AT FIELD AND FAWCETT, WHICH COMBINES A WINE MERCHANTS, DELICATESSEN AND CAFÉ ON ONE FAMILY FARM.

Field and Fawcett is a wine merchants and delicatessen within a converted barn on Cathryn's family farm, which has been providing customers with perfect pairings since 2006. The Café at Field and Fawcett was added in 2016 as part of the company's continuing development, under the knowledgeable management of Peter and Cathryn Fawcett. The three elements of the venture work as harmoniously as any great food and drink match; the kitchen uses as much produce as possible from the deli and the wine merchants – which also stocks an extensive range of spirits and local beers – is on hand to provide the pièce de résistance.

Peter has worked in the industry since leaving university, and has built up an international appreciation and understanding of wine from around the globe, picking up influences from Italy and New Zealand along the way which have led to corresponding specialities at Field and Fawcett. The deli also cherry-picks European meats and cheeses to go alongside its British offerings, so when it came to creating a menu for the café, Cathryn decided not to stray too far from home comforts. Good British fare is the order of the day, with monthly specials complementing the lunch and breakfast options for daytime dining.

Following this theme, The Café at Field and Fawcett uses local suppliers to create hearty dishes featuring meats from M&K Butchers, fish from Cross of York and bread from Haxby Bakehouse. There is a nod to the further flung culinary horizons explored at the deli, and of course an extensive – and very good value – wine list to accompany your meal. With lots of crossover between the café, deli and wine merchants, Field and Fawcett has become even more of a destination which continues to evolve under Peter and Cathryn's direction, supported by a team that they couldn't do without.

With big plans for the future, it's important for the business to be grounded in hands-on experience and lots of knowledge, so there are plenty of people to help customers find their way around the wine selection as well as the amazing range of spirits from whiskies to gins and rum to tequila. There's also a fair few Yorkshire beers, so you'd be hard pushed not to find your favourite tipple. With everything in one place, Field and Fawcett certainly has your wine and cheese night sorted, but much more besides, not to mention a great breakfast or lunch to set you up for a shopping trip!

COUNTRY PORK TERRINE WITH CORNICHONS AND TOASTED SOURDOUGH BREAD

A French classic made with the finest Yorkshire ingredients, using meat from the long-established M&K butchers on Bishopthorpe Road and sourdough bread from Haxby Bakehouse.

200g rindless pork shoulder

200g pork belly

150g pig's liver

2 tsp peppercorns

2 tsp juniper berries

100g rindless unsmoked streaky bacon, chopped into small pieces

1 tsp minced garlic

1 orange, zested and juiced

30ml French brandy

2 tbsp fresh chopped sage

1 tsp dried thyme

65g shelled pistachios

1 tsp fine sea salt

265g rindless smoked streaky, to line tin

TO SERVE

Cornichons

Mixed leaves

Sourdough toast

Mince the pork shoulder, pork belly and pig's liver together. You can ask your butcher to prepare this for you. Grind the peppercorns and juniper berries together with a pestle and mortar.

Combine all the ingredients except the smoked streaky bacon which lines the tin and place them in the fridge for a couple of hours to allow everything to infuse.

Meanwhile, line a 1lb loaf or terrine tin with the smoked streaky bacon, making sure each piece overlaps the next as you go. Leave enough bacon hanging over the edge to cover the top. If the bacon is a little thick you can stretch it out with the back of a knife.

Preheat the oven 150°c. Place the chilled terrine mix in the tin and bring the bacon over the top to cover the terrine. Cover the whole thing with parchment paper and foil then place the tin in a roasting tray. Add enough boiling water to come 2cm up the side of the tin. Cover the roasting tray with foil and place in the oven for 1 and a half to 2 hours, or if you have a meat thermometer until the internal temperature reaches above 90°c.

Once the terrine is cooked, remove the loaf tin from the roasting tin, take off the foil and parchment and replace with a fresh piece of parchment. Sit another loaf tin on top and weigh that down to compress the terrine. Chill in the refrigerator overnight.

Serve a slice of terrine on some mixed leaves with cornichons and toasted sourdough.

Preparation time: 30 minutes, plus 2 hour chilling | Cooking time: 1 ½-2 hours | Serves: 6

FOOD & DRINK PAIRINGS

WE'VE PUT TOGETHER SOME THOUGHTS ON THE BEST WINES TO ACCOMPANY SELECTED RECIPES FROM THIS BOOK, SO YOU CAN TURN ANY MEAL OR EVEN PUDDING INTO A SPECIAL OCCASION.

Eat Me Café – Lamb Meatballs with Endive, Shallots and Borlotti Beans

Valpollicella Ripasso, Le Arche, Veneto, Italy

Le Arche is a relatively new company, based in the Veneto region of north-east Italy. While traditional methods are respected, they are constantly updated with modern technology. This results in wines with old world complexity but added depth and richness of mid-palate fruit. This wine has intense aromas of fresh morello cherry and ripe plum. The palate has bright crunchy cherry-ish fruit with spicy vanilla notes and the classic bitter cherry finish typical of ripasso.

The Café at Field and Fawcett – Country Pork Terrine

'Le Clos' Rouge, Domaine Nizas, Languedoc, France

Domaine de Nizas is an organic winery creating elegant wines, which express the rich diversity of its terroirs on the heights of the medieval town of Pezenas. Smooth and sensual, this one reveals intense notes of red fruit. The personality between the fruits and spices of Syrah finds a balance between the sweetness of old Grenache and the vivacity of Mourvèdre, and delivers a definitively Mediterranean wine, generous and precise.

The Piebald Inn – The Yorkshire Coach Horse Pie

Brookby Hill Syrah, Two Rivers, Marlborough, New Zealand

Aromas of black peppercorn and charred meats combine with dried thyme and Herbes de Provence to create a botanical and savoury earthiness on the nose. The palate is in the leathery, earthy spectrum with blueberry and black fruit flavours shining through. This wine is bright and fresh with great concentration, focus and energy. A perfect match for the rich, savoury notes of this game pie.

Eat Me Café – Seared Steak and Egg Donburi

Marsanny, Pascal Marchand, Burgundy, France

A very pretty Marsannay. The nose has lovely subtle floral notes followed by a round, mouth-filling and velvety palate, full of all the classic Marsannay character. The finish is almost the most impressive part: long, and packed with sweet fruit. Rich enough to match the steak but subtle enough to handle the sweet and tangy rice bowl.

FOOD & DRINK PAIRINGS

WE'VE PUT TOGETHER SOME THOUGHTS ON THE BEST WINES TO ACCOMPANY SELECTED RECIPES FROM THIS BOOK, SO YOU CAN TURN ANY MEAL OR EVEN PUDDING INTO A SPECIAL OCCASION.

Ashley McCarthy Chocolate – Chocolate Florentines

Pedro Ximénez Sherry, Lustau, Spain

There is coffee, liquorice, sweet tobacco, prunes, figs, raisins, tea and a dozen other fleeting scents with a surprising lightness and delicacy here. An incredibly seductive and luscious drink.

Crumbs Cupcakery – Chocolate Orange Cupcakes

Myriad, Catherine Marshall, Elgin, South Africa

Chocolate and orange: a match made in heaven. This is a rare dessert-style, 100% Merlot. Sweet spiced plum and morello notes fill the glass, leading to a sumptuous and rich palate.

Shaun Rankin – Lamb with Jerusalem Artichoke and Ribblesdale Cheese

Rioja Reserva, Vina Cumbrero, Rioja, Spain

The highest quality tempranillo grapes from Rioja are carefully selected to craft this wine. Luscious red fruit flavours with elegant oak notes mingle with a lovely, concentrated palate.

Where the Ribbon Ends – Vanilla Cupcakes with Buttercream

L'Effronte, Moelleux, Domaine Matrot, Burgundy, France

L'Effronte is made from the grape variety Aligote. It offers a range of fresh fruit aromas such as quince, peach and apricot with a balance between sweetness and acidity. The richness of this wine derives from the concentration of the grapes thanks to beautiful sunny days between October and early November. A rare sweetie from Burgundy.

Jervaulx Abbey Tearoom – Carrot and Coconut Cake

Hukapapa Late Harvest Riesling, Marlborough, New Zealand

Rich golden colour gives a clue to what you're in for. The glass is filled with aromas of peach, tropical fruits as well as a hint of apple and citrus. The palate is bursting with luscious sweetness and a creamy texture, with refreshing lime acidity. Though sweet, it has a lovely clean, fresh finish.

Where the Ribbon Ends – Brownie Stacks

Ruby Dum, Niepoort, Douro, Portugal

Dominated by red cherries and plums with great freshness from ageing in large wooden vats, this wine is made by the charismatic and brilliant Dirk Niepoort. It's red in colour with a fresh vibrant aroma of dark fruits; a youthful wine with great balance, ready to drink with brownies.

Jervaulx Abbey Tearoom – Wensleydale, Ginger and Apricot Cheesecake

Natural Sweet Chenin, Perdeberg, Paarl, South Africa

The grapes are selected from 37 year old vines in the Perdeberg region and carefully aged in small French barrels. There are marmalade and honeycomb aromas with a hint of ginger, complementing the cheesecake beautifully. On the palate the wine is luscious and voluptuous.

Jervaulx Abbey Tearoom – Free-From Raspberry and Almond Cake

Moscato d'Asti, Saracco, Piemonte, Italy

This renowned winery run by Paolo Saracco is based in the village of Castiglione Tinella in an area called the Langhe Astigiane, widely regarded as the prime area for the production of Moscato d'Asti. The nose is of white peaches and fresh grapes, offering a creamy sweetness with lively citrus acidity. It would be perfect with this raspberry and almond cake but also as an aperitif. Moscato d'Asti deserves to be recognized as one of the world's greatest wines, simply for its capability to deliver pure sensorial pleasure.

Where The Ribbon Ends – Bespoke Cookies

Chardonnay Kreuth, Terlan

This Chardonnay displays deliciously ripe fruit with a hint of vanilla and toast on the finish. It has elegant complexity and a great length. A perfect choice to cut through the buttery cookies.

Restaurant EightyEight – Grilled Mackerel Kabayaki

Muscadet Sevre et Maine Sur Lie, Le Confluent, Chateau de L'Aulnaye, Loire, France

Mackerel is an oily fish and needs whites with crisp acidity. This Muscadet with its mineral, citrus-like taste is the perfect match.

Fletchers Restaurant – Braised Waterford Farm Beef Cheek

Two Left Feet, Mollydooker (Shiraz, Merlot and Cabernet Sauvignon), Mclaren Vale, Australia

Ripe fruits of dark cherry, blackberry, plum and raspberry are complemented by the secondary notes of vanilla and mixed spices. The silky satin-like fruit profile, encompassed by lovely ripe tannins, cascades effortlessly through the palate providing fantastic depth and a WOW factor.

The York Roast Co – War of the Roses

Chianti DOCG, Il Fortino, Tuscany, Italy

The benchmark wine style of Tuscany. Supple, sweet and sour cherry fruit with a hint of spice. The fresh acidity perfectly offsets the slight fattiness of the lamb.

FOOD & DRINK PAIRINGS

WE'VE PUT TOGETHER SOME THOUGHTS ON THE BEST WINES TO ACCOMPANY SELECTED RECIPES FROM THIS BOOK, SO YOU CAN TURN ANY MEAL OR EVEN PUDDING INTO A SPECIAL OCCASION.

The Bishy Weigh – Minestrone and Homemade Bread

Côtes du Rhône, Le Galetière, Jean Loron, France

Vineyards producing this Cotes-du-Rhone are planted on soils of rolled pebbles which come from the former bed of the Rhone river. The winery is fully organic. This wine offers beautiful notes of ripe fruit, raspberry and cherry but also prune, liquorice and a touch of violet. The mouth is round, with discreet soft tannins.

The Bishy Weigh – Mushroom Risotto with Roast Squash

Pinot Gris, Marcel Deiss, Alsace, France

There's nothing more warming than a delicious creamy, earthy risotto. Marcel Deiss is producing wines of great intensity and varietal definition. Ripe and voluptuous stone fruits work brilliantly with the butternut squash, while the fresh acidity is the ideal counterpoint to the earthy mushroom element of the dish.

The Whippet Inn and Love Cheese – Beef Rib Curry and Yorkshire Halloumi Saag Paneer

Pinotage, David and Nadia Sadie, South Africa

Arguably the best Pinotage in South Africa, this charming expression is turning heads and bringing people back to this unloved grape variety. Delicate red fruit, raspberry and cherry with an earthy undertone, aromatic, saline and rocky with a firm but fresh structure. Complements the spice in two elements of the dish.

Beadlam Grange – Blue Cheese Steak Burger

Crois Malbec, Susana Balbo, Mendoza, Argentina

The Crios Malbec from Susana Balbo is an excellent, pure and balanced red wine from the Argentinean wine-growing region of Mendoza. The expressive bouquet reveals notes of juicy blackberries, ripe cherries and crushed blueberries, discreetly accompanied by floral notes of violet and vanilla. On the palate this wine has a wonderful balance between the dark fruitiness and the silky tannin structure. The balanced body is beautifully captured by the fresh character of this Argentine red wine. Steak and Malbec: a match made in heaven.

The Bishy Weigh – Sticky Toffee Crumble Cake with Custard

Rutherglen Liqueur Muscat, Stanton & Killeen, Victoria, Australia

This wine is a fresh young style showing the sweet luscious fruit flavours for which Rutherglen Muscat is famous. Blended from wines that are three to five years old, it is fresh with notes of orange and intense raisin-like flavours. Rich, unctuous and perfect with sticky toffee.

RELAXED ELEGANCE

FONDLY KNOWN AS THE GRANTLEY ARMS FOR MANY YEARS, THE GRANTLEY BAR AND RESTAURANT HAS GRADUALLY TRANSFORMED INTO ONE OF NORTH YORKSHIRE'S HIDDEN CULINARY GEMS.

Valerie and Eric took the reins at the 17th-century Grantley Arms back in 2001, charmed by its historical features and stunning location in High Grantley, a picturesque village between Ripon and Pateley Bridge. Over the next 18 years, they put their stamp on the business, transforming it from village pub to dining destination – and it is now known as The Grantley Bar and Restaurant, more fittingly reflecting their food-led approach.

Valerie heads up the kitchen, while Eric is in charge of front of house. Eric is well known for always having time for a chat, whether it's with their many regulars or one of the holiday-makers who arrive to dine thanks to word-of-mouth recommendations. Between them, they've forged a reputation as being a friendly local that serves the very best in home-cooked food.

In the kitchen Val puts her passion for cooking into practice. She is a true foodie – she has always got her nose in a new cookbook looking for inspiration, and she loves experimenting with recipe development and learning about flavours. This passion comes to life in the kitchen where they make everything from scratch, right down to the bread, chutneys, sauces, ice creams and sorbets.

The menu changes all the time, depending on what seasonal ingredients are available locally. Their belly pork served with perfect crackling is a real favourite – 8 hours of slow-cooking leaves it sumptuously tender, then it's picked and pressed so you only get the very best of the meat. And the all-important crackling is cooked separately to ensure success.

"People come out for a treat, so it's important that they get to enjoy food that they can't easily make at home. Our triple-cooked chips, for example, are always popular, as is our battered fish – the batter is made with Yorkshire lager, and it's crisp and flavoursome." Valerie likes to keep the menu fresh, adding dishes like Thai green curry or fish risotto to the à la carte.

Crisp white table linens in the restaurant give the room a sense of elegance while still feeling warm and inviting. This is fine dining in the informal surrounds of a 17th-century pub. There is no pressure and no rush – Eric and Valerie want everyone to relax and enjoy their visit.

GRANTLEY BREAD AND BUTTER PUDDING

This is one of our favourite puddings. It's not on the menu all the time, but every time it's been on the menu and we take it off again, people are always asking where it has gone!

Butter, softened, for greasing and spreading

60g sultanas

60g raisins

4 tbsp dark rum

600ml double cream, plus extra to serve

1 vanilla pod

6 eggs

6 tbsp caster sugar

Approx. 10 slices medium sliced white bread

1 whole nutmeg

Grease an ovenproof tin or dish with butter. Put the sultanas, raisins and rum in a pan and leave in a warm place until all the rum has been soaked up by the fruit.

Put the cream and split vanilla pod into a separate pan and bring just to the boil. Hand-whisk the eggs in a heatproof bowl and then whisk in the sugar. Pour the boiling cream into the egg mix and whisk in. Set aside to cool.

Remove the crusts from each slice of bread and butter. Spread the slices out on a board and cut each slice into four triangles. Grate the whole nutmeg over them, then set aside.

When the custard has cooled, pass it through a fine sieve.

Pour a layer of custard into the greased dish, sprinkle on the soaked fruit, then add a layer of the bread. Repeat the process twice, so that there are three layers, ending with the bread. Gently press the bread a little, so that it goes slightly into the custard. Leave it to rest for 2 to 3 hours.

Preheat the oven to 130°c. Place the pudding into the preheated oven and bake for 30 minutes. When you are ready to serve, sprinkle each portion with demerara sugar and bake at 180°c for 15 minutes. Serve with double cream.

Preparation time: 20 minutes, plus 2-3 hours resting | Cooking time: 45 minutes | Serves 8

THE
BEST OF BOTH WORLDS

GRANTLEY HALL IS A MODERN CONCEPT INSIDE A GEORGIAN MANSION, BRINGING THE VIBRANCY OF THE CITY CENTRE TO THE BEAUTIFUL NORTH YORKSHIRE COUNTRYSIDE WITH A TANTALISING ARRAY OF DRINKING AND DINING OPTIONS.

Over the centuries, Grantley Hall has hosted celebrities, politicians and royalty: now this 17th century building, set in the picturesque North Yorkshire countryside, has opened its doors to guests as a luxury five star hotel and wellness retreat. The hotel launched in July 2019 and offers an indulgent sanctuary from the hectic pace of life. Grantley Hall is a Grade II* listed Georgian mansion that is steeped in history, and overflowing with opportunities for dining, drinking and relaxing in stunning settings. Emphasis is on the visitor's whole experience, and they have the choice of three very different restaurants to try, each headed up by impressive chefs.

Open seven days a week for breakfast, lunch and dinner, Fletchers Restaurant is characterised by oak panelling and open fireplaces, lending an intimate feel to the space. Award-winning head chef Craig Atchinson designs the menu, offering British and European choices, and – as with all Grantley's restaurants – there is a focus on showcasing local produce, such as seasonal berries grown by former businessman-turned-farmer John Briggs. Located in the original Queen Anne wing, diners can enjoy views of the beautiful surrounding parkland as they tuck into modern British cuisine.

Next up is Shaun Rankin which takes you on a culinary journey; this is fine dining at its best. As a proud Yorkshireman, Shaun enjoys hand-picking local suppliers when creating his menus. Whether it's vegetables and herbs from Grantley Hall's very own kitchen garden or organic meat from nearby farms, Shaun embraces all the high quality produce North Yorkshire has to offer. This elegant restaurant combines seasonal ingredients with Shaun's signature twist to create an experience that will stay with you all year round.

EightyEight is a bar and restaurant with an emphasis on fusion food and drink, where the fast-paced cities of the Far East meet the rolling North Yorkshire countryside. Whether you're enjoying a cocktail against a backdrop of beautiful Japanese gardens or tasting chef Ben Iley's authentic Pan-Asian cuisine, EightyEight is a unique experience, much like the special house blend gin it serves which is distilled at Raisethorpe Manor and uses homegrown botanicals including coriander, Japanese sansho pepper and cinnamon.

With such a diverse range of drinking and dining opportunities, coupled with beautiful gardens and grounds, Grantley Hall offers all the choice of the city amid the stunning Yorkshire Dales, bringing the best of both worlds together like nowhere else.

GRILLED MACKEREL KABAYAKI

A take on the traditional Japanese dish that is usually made with eel, but here uses the more widely available and popular fish, mackerel. Kabayaki means to open/flatten and grill, so a whole mackerel opened and deboned is a great substitute. The spicy citrus kosho paste really adds zing to the dish. Recipe by head chef Ben Iley.

4 mackerel, head removed and split with spine and bones removed or filleted
Splash of vegetable oil
100g watercress
30ml sesame oil
10g mixed sesame seeds, toasted

FOR THE PASTE

½ tsp yuzu kosho (available at most Chinese Supermarkets or online)
OR
10 oranges, zested
1 bird's eye chilli
50g salt

FOR THE GLAZE

250ml shoyu (Japanese soy sauce)
150ml mirin (Japanese sweet cooking sake)
100ml sake (Japanese rice wine)
100g sugar
1 thumb-size piece of ginger, peeled

FOR THE PASTE

If making your own kosho paste, start by finely grating the oranges, being extra careful not to get any of the bitter white pith from the orange.

Deseed the chilli and mince finely. Add the orange zest and the chilli to a pestle and mortar and work in the salt until you have a smooth paste. It might require a little a splash of orange juice and a touch of sugar if it is too harsh. Set aside until serving.

FOR THE GLAZE

Mix all the ingredients in a small pan and heat until boiling, then turn down to a high simmer and leave the glaze to reduce to a syrup consistency, more maple syrup than golden. Strain through a sieve and leave to cool.

Place the mackerel skin side up, brush with a little oil and season with salt, then grill under a medium heat until the skin is starting to crisp. Turn the fish and brush the flesh with the glaze before returning to the grill for a minute or two at most, not fully cooking the fish through. Turn the fish again and brush the skin with the glaze before returning to the grill, this time on high heat until the glaze becomes sticky and the skin nicely crisped. Leave to rest just for a minute. Dress the washed watercress with the sesame oil, a pinch of salt and the sesame seeds.

TO SERVE

Lay the fish down skin side up and use the very tip of a teaspoon to dab little dots of the kosho paste around the skin of the fish, to get little bursts of citrus heat as you eat. Spoon a little of the glaze around the plate and serve the dressed watercress on the side.

Preparation time: 10 minutes | Cooking time: 10 minutes | Serves 4

LAMB WITH JERUSALEM ARTICHOKE AND RIBBLESDALE CHEESE

This lovely elegant dish combines roasted Yorkshire lamb rack with sweet and succulent Jerusalem artichokes, tangy goats' cheese and a rich sauce to bring everything together.

FOR THE LAMB RACK

1 lamb rack
30g butter

FOR THE BRINE

1 ½ litres water
225g salt
75g sugar

FOR THE LAMB SAUCE

200g lamb bones, chopped finely
1 shallot
1 garlic bulb
Few white peppercorns and coriander seeds
Few sprigs of thyme and rosemary
Few bay leaves
Pinch of rock salt
100g white wine
5g sherry vinegar
300g chicken stock

FOR THE ARTICHOKE FOAM

900g Jerusalem artichokes
340g Ribblesdale cheese
340g milk
20g truffle honey
1g xanthan gum

FOR THE ARTICHOKE HASH

Bunch of chervil, tarragon and dill

FOR THE LAMB RACK

Clean any excess meat off the bones and remove any white sinew to expose the eye muscle. Whisk the ingredients for the brine together until the salt and sugar have fully dissolved, then place the lamb racks in the brine and leave for 1 hour. Remove the lamb from the brine and leave to dry.

Cook the lamb rack in an oven at 50°c for around 2 hours, then transfer it to a hot pan and sear to crisp up the skin. Add the butter with some rosemary and garlic cloves. Baste constantly for 30 seconds with foaming butter. Rest the lamb on a rack inside the oven for 4 to 5 minutes.

FOR THE LAMB SAUCE

Roast the lamb bones in a wide-bottomed saucepan until well coloured. Add the shallot, half the garlic bulb, spices, herbs and salt then cook until sweated. Deglaze the pan with the wine and sherry vinegar and reduce right down. Top up with the chicken stock and cook for 1 hour. Pass the sauce through a fine sieve and reduce it slightly, then drop in some garlic cloves and rosemary. Leave to infuse for 5 minutes, then pass the sauce through a double layer of wet muslin into a jug.

FOR THE ARTICHOKE FOAM

Steam the artichokes whole in their skins at 110°c with some vegetable oil and salt, until they are soft and the skins are loose. Cut them in half and peel off the skins using your thumb and finger. Reserve four or five tablespoons of flesh for the artichoke hash. Dry out the skins in a very low oven (around 55°c is ideal) until completely dry. This may take up to 3 hours. Crisp up the skins by frying them in oil at 180°c.

Grate the cheese, reserving two tablespoons for the artichoke hash. Warm the remaining cheese, milk and truffle honey together then add these to the warm artichoke flesh. Blend this mixture with the xanthan gum until very smooth. Pass the mixture through a fine sieve and whip the foam.

FOR THE ARTICHOKE HASH

Pick the leaves from the herbs, discarding the stalks, and roughly chop them. Warm the reserved artichoke flesh in a pan with a little oil, crushing slightly with a spoon. Stir in the reserved goats' cheese, season with salt, add about half a teaspoon of truffle honey then finish with the herbs. Keep this warm until serving.

TO SERVE

Plate the rested lamb rack with the artichoke hash in the crispy artichoke skins, then finish with the sauce and a spoonful of artichoke foam.

Preparation time: 1 hour 30 minutes | Cooking time: 4 hours | Serves: 4

BRAISED WATERFORD FARM BEEF CHEEK

Beef cheeks are an amazingly tasty cut that melts in the mouth and doesn't break the bank. All our meat is sourced or produced by Ryan Atkinson at R&J's: Yorkshire's finest farmers and butchers. All their animals graze freely in open pastures, an approach which is not only much kinder to the animals, but which also produces the highest quality meats that are rich in flavour. Recipe by head chef Craig Atchinson.

FOR THE BRAISED CHEEKS

4 beef cheeks, sinew removed

500ml red wine

2 cloves of garlic

1 bunch of fresh thyme

1 bay leaf

2 litres beef stock

FOR THE PEARL BARLEY RISOTTO

200g pearl barley

1 litre chicken stock

100ml double cream

200g parsley

30g parmesan, grated

Few drops of lemon juice

Salt, to taste

FOR THE GARNISH

2 small Roscoff onions

500g curly kale

FOR THE BRAISED CHEEKS

Put the beef cheeks in a suitable container, cover with the wine and add the garlic, thyme and bay leaf. Leave for at least 6 hours to marinate. Strain off the cheeks but keep the liquid. Transfer the marinade into a large pan and bring to the boil. In a hot frying pan, brown the beef cheeks until well caramelised on both sides. Add the cheeks to the stock pan with the marinade and cover with beef stock. Bring to the boil and simmer for around 4 hours or until the cheeks are very tender. Skim any scum or fat from the surface as it braises to keep the stock clean. When they are done, remove the cheeks from the stock and reduce it rapidly until thick and gelatinous. Put the cheeks back into the pan with the reduced stock and glaze the cheeks with the sticky reduction. Keep warm until needed.

FOR THE PEARL BARLEY RISOTTO

Put the chicken stock in a large pan and bring to the boil. Add the barley and boil for 12 minutes then transfer the barley into a medium-sized saucepan. Bring the double cream to the boil and add the parsley. Cook the parsley for 1 minute and then blend the mixture in a food processor until smooth. Pour the parsley cream onto the barley and heat on a medium flame. Just before serving add the parmesan, lemon juice and salt to your taste.

TO GARNISH

Slice the Roscoff onions into 1cm rings with the skin still on to hold them together. Brown the onions on each side in a frying pan with a little oil. Transfer into the oven set at 170°c for 12 minutes until cooked through.

Clean the kale in cold water and remove any woody stalk, then tear the kale leaves into smaller pieces if necessary. Put a knob of butter in a medium hot saucepan, then when the butter starts to foam add the kale and wilt for 1 to 2 minutes. Add a little salt to taste.

TO SERVE

Spoon some of the barley risotto onto the centre of the plate. Put the glazed cheek on top of the risotto. Arrange the onions and kale around the plate then drizzle the sauce over the tender cheek. This dish will really impress your friends and family and it's very cheap to produce.

Preparation time: 1 hour, plus 6 hours marinating | Cooking time: 4 hours | Serves 4

REAL BREAD

AN ARTISAN BAKERY ON THE OUTSKIRTS OF YORK, HAXBY BAKEHOUSE USES TRADITIONAL SLOW FERMENTATION METHODS IN THE PRODUCTION OF ITS AWARD-WINNING HANDMADE LOAVES.

Haxby Bakehouse was opened 11 years ago by husband and wife team Phil and Tina Clayton, with the aim of bringing "real bread" to the people of York. They took over an old health food store, with a small bakery in the back, when its owner was retiring – jumping head first into an opportunity to make their dream a reality.

Phil, a passionate baker who had been baking as a hobby for many years, went off to learn the essentials of sourdough with Andrew Whitley in the lake District, before returning to York to kick-start the new bakery. He began by changing the way the old bakery operated. He tracked down local organic flour producers and set about creating loaves that were free from artificial flour improvers, preservatives or emulsifiers.

Phil and his team focus on sourdoughs, for which they have picked up lots of awards over the years thanks to their slow-fermentation methods. They use low-yeasted overnight sponges, natural sourdough levain or a combination of the two, and all the breads are made with organic flour from Yorkshire Organic Millers, Stringers of Driffield and Shipton Mill. It's a time-consuming three-day process, but it gives the most flavoursome results.

They supply their award-winning bread to lots of restaurants, delis and shops in the area, too, including Michelin-starred The Black Swan.

At the weekend, they turn their hands to croissants and pastries – and the reputation of these has grown so fast, they have people waiting for them to come out of the oven on a Saturday morning.

The front of the premises is now a mouth-watering Yorkshire deli. It was transformed by Tina when they took over the shop 11 years ago and today boasts a huge selection of fine local produce. Tina has worked hard over the years to track down the best small producers and has built really strong relationships with local suppliers. Think organic milk and butter from Acorn Dairy, charcuterie from Lishmans of Ilkley, smoked fish and chicken from Staal Smokehouse, Voakes pies, a range of Yorkshire cheeses and home-baked ham.

They also sell locally roasted coffee, which is now available for people to sit down and enjoy on the premises. Coffee and a freshly baked croissant on a Saturday morning? What could be better!

HAXBY
BAKEHOUSE

PEAR &
DAMSON
CRUMBLE
TART
£2·80

THORNTONS
SCOTCH
EGG
£2·50

PRICE LIST

CINNAMON
MORNING
BUNS

CIABATTA
£2·00

GRANARY
£1·70
400gr

OLIVE
PAIN
RUSTIQUE
£2·25

WHITE
CRUSTY
£1·70

PISTACHIO
+
COCONUT
FLAPJACK
£2·80

YORKSHIRE
ORGANIC
MILLERS
BREAD FLOUR

THE YORKSHIRE 85 SOURDOUGH

A beautiful organic sourdough made with 85% extraction stoneground flour from our local mill, Yorkshire Organic Millers.

FOR THE LEVAIN

80g stoneground organic white flour

80g water

20g sourdough culture

FOR THE DOUGH

750g organic stoneground white flour

600g lukewarm water

150g levain

15g salt

FOR THE LEVAIN

Feed your levain 12 to 16 hours before you want to bake. Mix the flour, water and sourdough culture by hand in a bowl. Cover and leave to ferment overnight.

FOR THE DOUGH

The next day, weigh the flour into a large bowl. Weigh the water into a separate bowl (1g of water is 1ml, but weighing is a lot more accurate than using a measuring jug). Add 500g of the water to the flour (reserve 100g) and mix until you have no dry flour. Cover with a cloth. Leave for 30 minutes until the dough has relaxed and is less sticky.

Add 150g of the levain (the remaining 30g will feed your next batch) and add the reserved 100g of water. Knead for 5 minutes – it's meant to be fairly wet and sticky, don't be tempted to add more flour. Add the salt and knead for another 3 to 4 minutes. We now start the bulk fermentation. Cover and leave the dough for 30 minutes somewhere warm.

We now fold the dough to strengthen it. Stretch each side of the dough up, bring into the middle, and cover over. Repeat these folds twice more at 30 minute intervals. 30 minutes after the last fold, we're ready to shape the dough.

Turn the dough out onto a clean floured worktop, and divide into two pieces, each approximately 750g. Bring the edges of the dough into the middle, forming a ball. Flip the dough over, so the seam is under the ball. With practice you'll get more tension into the dough and a tighter shape. Leave to rest, covered, for 15 to 20 minutes.

Flour one-third of the dough and, using your hand or a rolling pin, flatten this area. Bring this flap over the top of the loaf. Now place the loaf flap-side down in a floured basket. Put the loaves somewhere warm for their final proof.

After 1½ to 2 hours they'll be ready to bake. They should be about half again in size. Preheat the oven to 220°c-230°c. For best results bake the loaves in a preheated casserole dish (or use an oven stone or baking tray).

Carefully tip the loaf flap-side up into the casserole dish. Put a lid on and place in the oven.

Bake for 25 minutes, then remove the lid and bake for another 10 minutes. Remember, crust is flavour. We like to bake this quite dark. Bien qui. The second loaf can be placed in the fridge while first loaf is baking. Now let your loaf cool. Enjoy!

Preparation time: 3 hours | Cooking time: 35 minutes | Makes: 2 loaves

LIFE IS WHAT YOU BAKE IT

JERVAULX ABBEY TEAROOM HAS BUILT UP A REPUTATION ON THE HOME BAKING DONE BY THE BURDON FAMILY, ALL IN AID OF PRESERVING THE INCREDIBLE ABBEY RUINS THEY OWN AND MAINTAIN.

Found in the picturesque Yorkshire Dales not far from Ripon, Jervaulx is one of the largest privately-owned Cistercian abbeys in the UK maintained solely by its owners. 2021 will be the 50th anniversary of this ownership, and 2019 saw the 25th year of opening for Jervaulx Abbey Tearoom. It has been a real labour of love for the Burdons, who continue to preserve and celebrate the atmospheric abbey ruins through hard work and lots of delicious home baking and cooking in the family-run business.

Carol and her husband Ian began the venture in 1994 and were later joined by their daughters, Anna and Gayle, who brought new skills but also a genuine love for the place back with them. Having grown up around the cakes their mum baked, the sisters developed the tearoom even further and Gayle started her own bespoke wedding and celebration cake business, Where The Ribbon Ends. Run from the tearoom, this business is also a family affair and has won industry awards.

"From its opening, I wanted to base the tearoom on home baking and good food that was locally sourced wherever possible," says Carol. As time went on, it became apparent that there was a need to meet dietary requirements too, especially for those who are vegan, gluten- or dairy-free, so

Carol developed a range of cakes combining her traditional baking with new trends to suit all visitors.

The key focus has always been on freshly made food – whether sweet or savoury – so using ingredients sourced locally from producers around Yorkshire is important to the Burdons. Ian also likes to lend a hand by popping up to the kitchen with fruit and vegetables from his garden to challenge Carol, Gayle and Anna. Seasonal gluts account for the creation of some of their favourite cakes, and the range of pickles they make, including Beetroot Relish and Wensleydale Beer Chutney, jars of which are also sold in the gift section within the tearoom.

Food and drink has always been central to the abbey, whose original inhabitants produced cheese now recognised as a precursor to the famous Wensleydale variety made nearby. The Burdon family still place great emphasis on supporting local food and drink businesses that produce unique ingredients in the county they love, and are proud to be preserving the abbey together through their love for home baking and cooking at Jervaulx Abbey Tearoom.

FREE-FROM RASPBERRY AND ALMOND CAKE

Raspberries and almonds are a match made in heaven, especially when you're baking with them – the aroma is just heavenly – but the best thing about this award-winning cake is that nobody guesses it's gluten and dairy-free. This cake was awarded 'Best Free From Product 2017' by Deliciously Yorkshire.

170g dairy-free spread

170g caster sugar

½ tsp vanilla extract

3 large eggs

85g wheat and gluten-free self-raising flour

1 tsp xanthan gum

½ tsp gluten-free baking powder

115g ground almonds

170g fresh or frozen raspberries

Preheat the oven to 180°c and line the base of a 20cm deep-sided round tin with baking parchment.

Cream the dairy-free spread, caster sugar and vanilla extract together until light and fluffy. Gradually add the eggs one at a time. Don't worry if the mixture starts to curdle. Slowly fold in the flour, xanthan gum, baking powder and ground almonds, taking care not to knock out the air. Gently fold in the raspberries, taking care not to break them up. Spoon the mixture into the prepared tin and level out with the back of a spoon.

Bake for 1 hour and 15 minutes, or until a skewer comes out clean from the centre of the cake, so check it after 1 hour. Remove the cake from the oven when done and leave to cool.

Dust with icing sugar just before serving. This cake is delicious with dairy-free ice cream, and freezes well if you're not going to eat it on the day.

Preparation time: 10 minutes | Cooking time: 1 hour 15 minutes | Serves: 8

WENSLEYDALE, GINGER AND APRICOT CHEESECAKE

This delicious cheesecake is a welcome taste of the Yorkshire Dales. This recipe has been with us for over 20 years; it's really easy to make and gives such a lovely flavour. It's perfect on its own, or you can serve it with cream for a real indulgence.

FOR THE BASE

170g margarine

455g biscuits, crumbed

FOR THE CHEESECAKE

340g full-fat cream cheese

55g sugar

340g Wensleydale cheese, grated

85g apricots, chopped

2 pieces of stem ginger, finely chopped

4 tbsp cream

Line the base of a 23cm round cake tin with greaseproof paper.

FOR THE BASE

Gently melt the margarine, then add the biscuit crumbs and mix with a wooden spoon. Pour into the base of the tin and press down to create a firm base.

FOR THE CHEESECAKE

Put the cream cheese into a mixing bowl and beat well. Add the sugar, Wensleydale cheese, apricots and ginger. Mix well and add one tablespoon of cream at a time. When it's completely mixed, pour into the tin and press firmly down with a spatula. Chill overnight in the fridge to set the cheesecake.

Preparation time: 15 minutes | Chilling time: 12 hours | Serves: 10

CARROT AND COCONUT CAKE

This carrot cake is often used for wedding cakes with Where The Ribbon Ends; the coconut adds a great texture while the sultanas retain moisture. With a delicious soft and sweet cream cheese icing, it becomes irresistible.

FOR THE CAKE

4 eggs
340g soft brown sugar
280ml sunflower oil
400g plain flour
100g desiccated coconut
2 tsp ground cinnamon
2 tsp bicarbonate of soda
400g carrots, grated
200g sultanas

FOR THE CREAM CHEESE ICING

230g cream cheese, chilled
230g butter, at room temperature
450g icing sugar

FOR THE CAKE

Preheat the oven to 170°c and line the sides and the base of a 23cm round cake tin.

Beat the eggs and sugar together at high speed until the mixture becomes thicker and paler. Continue to beat for a few more minutes before slowly pouring the oil in a steady stream into the mixture, while beating at high speed. The mixture should hold the shape of the trail as the whisk is lifted up when all the oil has been incorporated.

Add all of the dry ingredients and mix on a slow speed until they're evenly distributed. Stir in the grated carrots and sultanas. Pour the mixture into the cake tin and bake for 1 hour 30 minutes or until a skewer comes out clean.

FOR THE CREAM CHEESE ICING

Beat all of the ingredients together for 3 to 5 minutes at high speed until pale. Make sure all the butter has been incorporated properly.

TO FINISH

Once the cake has completely cooled, slice the cake through the middle and add the cream cheese icing to sandwich the cake together and cover the top, then decorate as you wish.

Preparation time: 15 minutes | Cooking time: 1 hour 30 minutes | Serves: 10

FOR THE LOVE OF CHEESE

A CHEESE SHOP LIKE NO OTHER, LOVE CHEESE IS A HAVEN FOR CHEESE LOVERS…
WITH A WIDE RANGE OF CHEESE FROM YORKSHIRE AND FURTHER AFIELD, AND
A COSY CAFÉ AND GARDEN IN WHICH TO ENJOY THEM.

When Harry and Phoebe Baines took over Love Cheese on 15th September 2015 they could see the potential in the little shop to create something truly special. They immediately set about transforming the business into York's only specialist cheese shop and café.

The first big change was to focus on buying as directly as possible from independent producers. They now work with an array of dairies and creameries, both locally and across the country, as well as a French maturer, so that they can offer an extensive choice of Yorkshire, British and continental cheeses.

They soon earned themselves a reputation for putting together stunning cheese tower wedding cakes – they now make about 40 every year – as well as setting up an online shop to reach a wider audience.

Harry and Phoebe have made the most of the shop's setting, nestled beneath the ancient city walls on Gillygate. As well as a cosy little café inside, there is a little cheese oasis outside, in the form of a well-furnished garden, that sits right underneath the famous city wall. It's no wonder Love Cheese has become a firm favourite for both locals and tourists to stop and have a bite to eat.

They serve cheeseboards made to order – choose three, four or five cheeses, accompanied by bread or crackers and local chutney. Ideal with a glass of fine wine from their selection. They also serve grilled cheese sandwiches ranging from The Classic (mature cheddar, red Leicester and mozzarella – add pesto, if you like) to Sweet Chilli Halloumi or Blue Cheese and Red Onion Relish. And the cheese really does take the starring role in the toasties, filled to the brim and oozing out of the side.

Love Cheese hosts a series of events in the shop, too. Private cheese tastings are 2-hour experiences that cover things like red wine and cheese, bubbles and brie, or even beer and cheese matching. They also host a semi-regular Discover series (Discover Italy, Discover France or Discover the UK, for example), where guests can immerse themselves into the wine and cheese culture of a country through a carefully crafted tasting menu. Bringing people together to share good food and wine is exactly what Love Cheese is all about.

LOVE CHEESE

Shop & Café

LOVE CHEESE

LOVE CHEESE
CAFE AND
GARDEN

← THIS WAY

ROSEBUD PRESERVES
MASHAM, YORKSHIRE

Great Yorkshire
Pickle

SQUEAKY
cheese
ORIGINAL
220g

A TASTE OF YORKSHIRE

THE WHIPPET INN HAS BEEN FLYING THE FLAG FOR YORKSHIRE PRODUCE FROM DAY ONE! ITS REPUTATION FOR SERVING THE BEST LOCAL BEEF, PAIRED WITH CRAFT ALES, WINE AND GIN PRODUCED THROUGHOUT THE REGION, HAS ATTRACTED RECOGNITION YEAR AFTER YEAR.

The Whippet Inn was opened by Martin Bridge and his business partner Andrew Whitney in 2013.

Martin had his eye on the Victorian red brick coach house for many years. When the "backstreet boozer", as it was at the time, came up for sale, the pair jumped at the chance to turn it into something special. Their aim was to showcase the best of Yorkshire's produce coupled with great hospitality – and The Whippet Inn was born.

Originally, dry-aged beef formed the core of the menu, making the restaurant stand out from the crowd. Six years later, mouth-watering beef still features on the main menu alongside spectacular special cuts and breeds, however today the choice is far more eclectic.

The Whippet Inn's carefully crafted menu features an array of delicious starters, such as lamb belly ham, served with whipped feta cheese, pomegranate, toasted hazelnuts and pomegranate molasses or cured sea trout, wrapped in sushi nori with charred pink grapefruit segments, squid ink prawn crackers, sea purslane and fennel.

Main courses include delightful dishes such as roast cod and merguez sausages with crispy shredded potato, roasted cherry tomatoes, padron peppers and dressed spinach leaves. You could even try one of many vegetarian dishes like the onion tarte tatin poached in Chardonnay with Yellisons goats'

curd, broad beans, peas, radish and asparagus in smoked garlic butter. Or of course one of the legendary steaks are always available.

Not only is The Whippet Inn one of York's best-loved restaurants, it is in fact York's original gin house and continues to maintain an approach to the drinks menu that sets it apart. They offer a diverse range of the county's best craft lagers and ales, sourcing wines from local companies to create an incredible wine list, boasting some fantastic sparkling wines produced here in England.

The Whippet Inn remains a true independent and has not veered from its original ethos of selecting local businesses when going about gathering the best that Yorkshire has to offer. Ensuring they have taken the time to create a menu, service and atmosphere that guests will return for time and again lies at the heart of what this restaurant does.

Love Cheese based on Gillygate in York is one of their most trusted suppliers when it comes to quality products, so it seemed obvious to work closely with their friends to produce the delectable dish in this book. Taking Yorkshire ingredients and transforming them into an unexpected, bold and flavoursome plate of food is synonymous with the award-winning Whippet Inn and truly sums up their culinary experience.

BEEF RIB CURRY AND YORKSHIRE HALLOUMI SAAG PANEER

Making a classic saag paneer using local Yorkshire halloumi from our friends at Love Cheese sums up the way we love to cook at The Whippet Inn. This recipe puts many Yorkshire suppliers at the heart of an Indian-inspired dish, from rapeseed oil to beef and cheese.

FOR THE SPICE MIX

4 tsp each coriander seeds, cumin seeds, paprika, turmeric and cayenne pepper

½ cinnamon stick

FOR THE BEEF

50ml Yorkshire rapeseed oil

4 beef short ribs (350g)

FOR THE SAUCE

2 medium onions

1 green pepper, deseeded

6 cloves garlic & 50g fresh ginger

2 fresh chillies, deseeded

400g tin chopped tomatoes

300ml beef stock

TO FINISH THE CURRY

1 handful coriander, chopped

2 lemons, juice and zest

100ml tamarind sauce

1 tsp garam masala

2 tsp sugar & 50g plain flour

FOR THE SAAG PANEER

2 cloves garlic & 50g fresh ginger

1 medium onion

1 chilli, deseeded

400g spinach, washed

50ml Yorkshire rapeseed oil

400g Yorkshire halloumi, cut into 2cm cubes

1 tsp turmeric & 1 tsp garam masala

100ml double cream

1 lemon, juice and zest

FOR THE SPICE MIX

In a dry pan, toast all the ingredients over a low heat for 3 to 4 minutes or until lightly browned. Transfer to a food processor/blender and blitz until combined. Set aside.

FOR THE BEEF

Combine half the spice mix with the oil and a pinch of salt, and rub over the beef. Cover and leave to marinate for at least 1 hour, but preferably overnight in the fridge. In a large frying pan, colour the beef on all sides, then move to an ovenproof dish. Set aside the used frying pan for later use. Preheat the oven to 180°c.

FOR THE CURRY SAUCE

Roughly chop the onions and pepper. Peel and chop the garlic and ginger. Add all the sauce ingredients (except the tomatoes and beef stock) with a pinch of salt to a food processor and blitz for 2 to 3 minutes until a coarse purée is formed. Transfer the purée and the remaining half of the spice mix to the frying pan, and cook over a medium heat for 10 minutes, stirring constantly. Add the tomatoes and beef stock, and bring to the boil, then pour over the beef. Cover and cook for 3 hours in the preheated oven until tender (timings may vary for fan-assisted ovens). Once cooked, remove the beef and return the sauce to a pan.

TO FINISH THE CURRY

Add the coriander, lemon juice and zest, tamarind, garam masala, sugar and flour to the sauce, and simmer for 10 minutes to cook out the flour. Return the beef ribs to the sauce.

FOR THE SAAG PANEER

Peel and mince the garlic and ginger. Finely slice the onion. Roughly chop the chilli. In a dry frying pan, cook the spinach over a low heat until wilted, then remove and pat dry before roughly chopping. Add half the oil to a pan over a medium heat, then add the halloumi and fry until golden on all sides. Remove and set aside. Add the remaining oil to the pan along with all the spices, the onion, chilli, garlic and ginger, and cook over a medium heat until slightly soft. Add the spinach and cheese back to pan, then add the cream and lemon, and simmer for 2 minutes to allow the mixture to combine.

TO SERVE

We recommend severing in large bowls in the centre of the table to allow everyone to dig in!

Preparation time: 30 minutes | Cooking time: 3 hours 30 minutes | Serves 4

ROASTED RACK OF LAMB WITH
SLOW COOKED BELLY AND OFFAL

*Well-cooked offal has lovely flavour and texture, so don't be afraid to try these
under-used cuts. The aniseed notes in the pastis cut through all the richness of this
dish nicely. A feast for lamb lovers!*

FOR THE BRAISED
LAMB BELLY

800g boneless lamb belly

Sea salt

1 garlic bulb, halved horizontally

*1 onion, carrot and stick of celery,
roughly chopped*

250ml red wine

1 litre lamb stock

5 rosemary sprigs

2 tsp mint sauce

15g capers, chopped

1 lemon, zested and juiced

FOR THE PASTIS JUS

100ml pastis

FOR THE LAMB RACKS
AND OFFAL

*4 two-bone lamb racks, skin removed and
scored*

*200g lamb sweetbreads, membrane
removed*

100g seasoned flour

1 egg, beaten

50g panko breadcrumbs

2 lamb kidneys, halved and cored

300g lamb liver, quartered

FOR THE BRAISED LAMB BELLY

Rub the lamb belly well with salt then seal it on both sides in a hot frying pan. Sear
the cut faces of the garlic bulb at the same time. Transfer both to an ovenproof
dish. Cook the chopped vegetables in the pan on a high heat until they start to
brown, then add them to the dish. Deglaze the pan with the red wine and pour that
into the dish with enough lamb stock to cover the lamb. Add the rosemary, cover
the dish and cook in the oven at 160°c for 3 to 4 hours until the lamb is tender.

Allow the meat to cool until it can be handled, then pass the remaining liquid
through a sieve, retaining the garlic. Place the liquid in the fridge to cool. Using
a fork, flake the lamb belly and remove any sinew or membrane from the meat.
Squeeze the soft garlic into the lamb and add the mint sauce, capers, lemon zest and
juice. Mix well and check the seasoning, adding salt if necessary. Roll the mixture
into a sausage shape roughly 2cm across using cling film, tie both ends and chill.

FOR THE PASTIS JUS

Remove any fat from the surface of the chilled cooking liquid, then combine it with
the pastis in a large saucepan. Reduce the sauce over a high heat until it is the right
consistency.

FOR THE LAMB RACKS AND OFFAL

In a large ovenproof frying pan, seal the seasoned lamb racks on all sides, making
sure to colour the fat well. Place the pan into the oven at 180°c for 10 minutes with
the lamb fat side down.

Remove the belly 'sausage' from the fridge, remove the cling film, cut into slices and
warm through in the oven.

Meanwhile, coat the sweetbreads in the seasoned flour, beaten egg and then
breadcrumbs. Remove the lamb racks from the pan, keeping any fat, and allow them
to rest somewhere warm. In the pan on a medium high heat, cook the offal. The
sweetbreads and kidney will need around 60 seconds on each side and the liver just
30 seconds each side. Allow to rest before serving.

TO SERVE

Carve each lamb rack into two cutlets and slice each piece of liver in half. Plate
with the other offal, pastis jus and some roasted shallots with blanched tenderstem
broccoli on the side.

Preparation time: 30 minutes | Cooking time: approx. 4 hours | Serves: 4

HEY JO COCKTAIL

You will need to make your sugar gomme or syrup in advance for this cocktail recipe, as it needs to cool before use. You will also need a cocktail shaker.

40ml sugar syrup
1 lime, halved
Ice
25ml Campari
25ml Tarquin's Strawberry & Lime Gin

To make the sugar syrup, combine equal parts boiling water and caster sugar in a small bowl. Stir until the sugar has dissolved, then set aside until completely cooled.

Put plenty of ice into your cocktail shaker and squeeze the juice of half the lime over it. Add the Campari, gin and cooled sugar syrup to the cocktail shaker. Shake vigorously.

Take a tumbler or rocks glass and add fresh ice to it. Pour the contents of the cocktail shaker over the ice through a strainer (usually there is one built into the shaker) to fill the glass.

Slice the other lime half into wedges, then add one or two depending on personal taste. To make the drink even more special, we like to add purple or even yellow viola flowers as a garnish, to match Jo's hair colour.

THIS RECIPE IS DEDICATED TO THE MEMORY OF JO O'KEEFFE.

In May of 2019 we sadly lost one of our 'Best Boys' to suicide. Jo was an amazing person and throughout the years represented our business as a fantastic server, bartender and lover of hospitality, with a genuine flair for looking after his guests and making them feel welcome. Jo was known for his giggle, terrible time keeping, bright hair and interesting fashion choices: just some of the reasons he was so special.

In his honour, we created a cocktail using some of Jo's favourite ingredients, to produce a drink that we know he would have been very proud of. We wanted to ensure that something good could come from Jo's death and so for every Hey Jo cocktail sold, we donate £1 to the charity CALM: Campaign Against Living Miserably. CALM is a leading movement against suicide, which is now the biggest killer of men under the age of 45 in the UK. They believe that anyone can hit a crisis point and they are here to help, running a free confidential helpline and webchat for anyone who needs to talk about life's problems. The charity was selected by Jo's family and everyone in his life now does everything they can to help raise the profile of CALM on a daily basis.

We will be raising money for CALM by selling this book; any profit made by The Whippet Inn will be donated directly to the charity and its ongoing mission to Campaign Against Living Miserably.

CALM: www.thecalmzone.net or 0800-58-58-58

Preparation time: 5 minutes | Serves 1

CRAFT GINS OF YORKSHIRE

INSPIRED BY THE CRAFT GIN REVOLUTION, NATURAL BOTANICALS AND LOCAL PRODUCE, NORTHERN FOX YORKSHIRE GINS ARE CREATING EXCITING NEW GINS THAT ARE INSPIRED BY THEIR YORKSHIRE ROOTS.

Northern Fox Yorkshire Gins officially began life in 2018, but its story goes back much further than that. Its founders Oliver and Aimée have known each other since they were teenagers, although it was many years and five children (three for Oliver and twins for Aimée) later that they came back together in their home county. A shared love of gin and a passion for flavour experimentation inspired a joint foray into the world of distilling.

Oliver, a microbiologist, had worked in the drinks industry for many years, and he shared a belief with Aimée that gins were best when made with natural flavours in small batches. Although they'd been inspired by the craft gin revolution, they were also a bit disillusioned by the way the terms 'craft' and 'artisan' had been hijacked by large-scale producers. They planned to bring the process back to basics with nothing artificial added to Fox Gins.

This approach can be seen in the carefully selected botanicals in their products. The classic Yorkshire Dry Gin uses only six botanicals – all natural – and you can taste every single one of them. The Traditional Pink Gin is a world away from other pink gins available. It's certainly not sweet; instead it blends the Yorkshire Dry Gin with Angostura bitters. The third gin, Liquorice Root Gin, pays homage to Yorkshire's traditional treat Pontefract cakes.

They have recently began making a special edition gin after a local farmer contacted them about his unusual fruit – honeyberries. They went to meet him, tasted them and were immediately won over. A cross between a gooseberry and a blueberry, these berries lend themselves perfectly to gin – and Northern Fox Yorkshire Gins are the only people making honeyberry gin in the country. Launched in summer 2019, this gin quickly became one of their most popular products.

Aimée and Oliver plan to keep their production methods artisan even as they grow. They have no intention of moving to larger stills. They plan to continue using small stills to make small batches, to hand-label all their bottles onsite and to sell through Yorkshire outlets and pubs, as well as showcasing Yorkshire Gin further afield. They are excited about experimenting with seasonal flavours to make limited edition releases and continuing to host gin and food pairings, masterclasses, and gin and cocktail bars.

They're evolving all the time, experimenting with flavours and building new relationships with other local businesses such as the one with Fest By Fire, where they hold regular supper nights. As they continue to grow, one thing is for sure, they'll be keeping their Yorkshire heritage at the very heart of Fox Gins.

LITTLE WOLD HONEYBERRY FIZZ

We have paired our exclusive Yorkshire honeyberry gin with a sparkling rosé wine from the amazing 'Little Wold Vineyard', whose grapes are grown on the hills of East Yorkshire in South Cave. These two unique drinks together create a stylish, crisp, classically Yorkshire aperitif cocktail that will start any night off perfectly.

25ml Northern Fox Yorkshire Honeyberry Gin

155ml Little Wold Vineyards 'Heathers Sparkle' Sparkling Rosé Wine (or any other dry sparkling rosé wine if not available)

Blackberry, to garnish

Add a blackberry to a sparkly champagne flute. Pour in a measure of Northern Fox Yorkshire Honeyberry Gin and then fill the flute to the top with the Sparkling Rosé Wine. Watch the blackberry spin and fizz. Drink and enjoy.

LITTLE WOLD HONEYBERRY FIZZ MARRIES WITH....

This cocktail is dry, crisp and refreshingly tart, so it works well with rich indulgent canapés or tapas with soft cheese, smoked fish and cured meats.

TASTING NOTES

We have partnered with a pioneering East Yorkshire farm, a founding UK grower of this berry, to create the UK's one and only honeyberry gin. The honeyberry is tart and sweet in equal measure, making this unique gin exceedingly different to anything else.

The aroma is fruity, with a beautiful sharpness arriving on the palate first to balance the sweetness which comes later and finishes with the zing of the peppercorns.

PERFECT SERVE

Serve with plenty of ice. A Fever-Tree light tonic results in a more tart drink while a Fever-Tree elderflower tonic brings out the sweetness of the berry. Garnish with lime.

Preparation time: 5 minutes | Serves 1

NORTHERN FOX YORKSHIRE DRY CLASSIC GIN & TONIC

Inspired by the refined methods of the 'London Dry Gin distillers'. Our original Yorkshire dry gin uses high-grade grain spirit and filtered Yorkshire water which is infused for 48 hours with six carefully selected natural botanicals. Pairing with a good-quality light tonic creates a beautifully smooth G&T.

Fresh-from-the-freezer ice cubes

50ml Northern Fox Yorkshire Dry Gin

150-200ml Fever-Tree Refreshingly Light Tonic

Slices of lime and a sprinkle of juniper berries, to garnish

Glass – Gin balloon glass

Fill a gin balloon glass to the top with ice. Pour in a double measure of Northern Fox Yorkshire Dry Gin. Fill to your liking with refreshingly light tonic water. Add 1 or 2 circles of fresh lime and a sprinkle of juniper berries (if you don't have the juniper don't worry). Stir, then sit back, relax and enjoy.

NORTHERN FOX YORKSHIRE DRY CLASSIC GIN & TONIC MARRIES WITH....

A clean and smooth G&T with floral, spicy and sweet layers it works well on the palate with lustrous foods such as duck, charcuterie and rich or spicy curries.

TASTING NOTES

Inspired by the refined methods of the London Dry Gin distillers, our original Yorkshire Dry Gin uses high grade British grain spirit and filtered Yorkshire water, which is infused for 48 hours with six carefully selected natural botanicals.

We haven't overloaded this gin with botanicals, carefully selecting our favourite ones to give this gin a classic taste, with every botanical flavour being present in its drinking. Juniper and coriander are at the forefront with spicy, sweet and citrus after notes.

PERFECT SERVE

Serve with lots of ice and a Fever-Tree light tonic. Garnish with lime.

Preparation time: 5 minutes | Serves 1

TRADITIONAL PINK GIN CRUSH

With the wave of current pink gins being sweet and fruity, we wanted to try something different and revive the 'Traditional Pink Gin Cocktail'. Fresh and bitter, with botanicals and spice – juniper, cinnamon and clove stand out, but there are many more flavours to decipher. Can you pick them out?

Fresh-from-the-freezer ice cubes

50ml Northern Fox Traditional Pink Gin (definitely a double)

200-300ml Fever-Tree Aromatic Tonic

Slice of orange, to garnish

Put the freshly cut orange slice in the bottom of a rocks or highball glass. Fill the glass to the top with ice. Pour in a good double of Northern Fox Traditional Pink Gin. Fill the glass to the top with aromatic tonic. Push in an environmentally friendly straw and agitate. Sip until relaxed.

TRADITIONAL PINK GIN CRUSH MARRIES WITH....

Having bitterness and spice in abundance, our traditional pink gin cocktail marries well with seafood, poultry or vegetable dishes with creamy or tomato-based sauces. Classic fruit desserts with crème fraîche or fresh cream also work well.

TASTING NOTES

With current 'Pink Gins' being sweet and fruity, we wanted to try something different and revive 'Traditional Pink Gin'.

This is achieved by blending our Yorkshire Dry Gin with Angostura bitters; a complex herbal brew that dates back centuries, made with many different botanicals that give it a deep and layered taste profile. Amazingly, only five people alive know the secret recipe and we love this heritage.

This gin has a clean, crisp, refreshing taste with notes of juniper, clove and cinnamon, though there are many more flavours to pick out.

PERFECT SERVE

Serve with lots of ice and a Fever-Tree aromatic tonic. Garnish with a slice of orange.

Preparation time: 5 minutes | Serves 1

LIQUORICE ESPRESSO MARTINI

Liquorice… in an espresso martini? Yes it is, and yes it works! This cocktail was created using our first Yorkshire flavoured gin – Northern Fox Liquorice Root Gin. Designed with the historical treat 'Pontefract Cakes' in mind, the flavour will bring back memories for delight or disdain from your childhood memories… either way it will be a talking point. This is a luxurious, frothy cocktail that looks stunning and has waves of coffee and liquorice and a good punch of aniseed.

Fresh-from-the-freezer ice cubes
50ml any good espresso or real coffee
37.5ml Northern Fox Liquorice Root Gin
25ml Borghetti Coffee liquor
12.5ml Monin Aniseed Syrup
1 star anise, to garnish

Fill a cocktail shaker with ice. Add in the double measure of espresso. Pour in 1 ½ measures of Northern Fox Liquorice Root Gin. Add in a measure of Borghetti and ½ a measure of Monin aniseed syrup. Close the shaker lid tightly, hold onto the bottom and the lid, and shake rigorously for at least 40 seconds to mix. Take off the lid and pour into a martini glass through a cocktail strainer; this helps to give a creamy, frothy head. Add a star anise in the centre to garnish. I know, it looks too beautiful to drink… but it tastes even better.

LIQUORICE ESPRESSO MARTINI MARRIES WITH….

This cocktail is delicious on its own, coffee-led with hits of liquorice and aniseed whilst also frothy and viscous. However, it works amazingly with desserts, or 'puddings' as we say in Yorkshire. Especially those with spices such as cinnamon and ginger.

TASTING NOTES

We created this flavour with the historical Yorkshire treat Pontefract Cakes in mind. This limited edition gin made with real liquorice root will bring back childhood memories of delight (or disdain) for that unique flavour. Either way, it will certainly be a talking point, though perhaps controversial.

This gin contains only three botanicals, which allows the liquorice flavour to be the star of the show. If it is tasted in two sips, the first flavour that comes through on the palate is the woodiness and earthiness of the root. With the second, the sweetness and anise of the liquorice sits on the tongue.

PERFECT SERVE

Serve in a balloon glass, with a Fever-Tree ginger beer and plenty of ice. Garnish with a slice of fresh ginger. This gives the drink fiery, woody and earthy notes at first then leaves a lasting, viscous, liquorice sweetness on the tongue.

Preparation time: 5 minutes | Serves 1

FAR FROM A ONE TRICK PONY

WITH MORE THAN 50 VARIETIES OF HANDMADE PIES AND A COLLECTION OF 100 GINS, THE PIEBALD INN DOESN'T SKIMP ON QUALITY OR QUANTITY WHEN IT COMES TO GOOD FOOD AND DRINK.

The story of The Piebald Inn starts before it even existed. Jon, the owner, was then running a smaller place in East Yorkshire and slowly but surely, he and his pie menu outgrew the pub. When he found a freehold up for sale in 2014 it was the perfect opportunity to start something new, with his friend and business partner Gary. The Piebald Inn was opened under The Pie Pub Company, which is something they hope to expand in the very near future.

Over the next five years the spacious building was extensively renovated, adding seven luxury bedrooms plus an expansive sun terrace and creating a large bar area as well as a stable-themed restaurant. Thanks to Jon and Gary's attentions, whether you want to stay over, relax with a drink or tuck into a hearty meal, The Piebald can accommodate you any day of the year.

Head chef Tony Sturgeon, who worked with Jon at the previous venue, makes sure each pie that leaves the kitchen is up to scratch, and produces an extravagant five course meal for Christmas Day (the only day pies aren't on the menu!) with his team. Although the different types of pie are named after breeds of horse, but the equestrian theme stops at the fillings! The Piebald Inn offers choices galore, from the traditional steak and kidney, chicken and mushroom, meat and potato and other recognisable pies to the more adventurous pork vindaloo, various game fillings and even a goat pie.

There is also a breakfast pie, eight vegetarian pies, four fish pies and even vegan pies available on request. Some customers are working their way through the 50-strong list, Jon says, and the pies' reputation has spread far and wide across Yorkshire and beyond simply by word of mouth.

The bar features six cask ales, an extensive wine list to suit all tastes, lagers on tap and over 100 varieties of gin, so there's no shortage of good stuff to chase your pie down with! The pub's garden (which the majority of rooms open out onto) is also a big attraction, which alongside the free pitches for motorhomes – providing the owners use the pub, of course – makes The Piebald Inn a self-contained destination that's ideal for, locals, holidaymakers and visitors from further afield who just have to try the pie!

THE YORKSHIRE COACH HORSE PIE

A traditional mixed game and pork pie, using seasonal locally sourced game and minced pork. A real treat for those autumnal and winter months.

1kg mixed game (venison, pheasant, pigeon etc.)

500g minced pork

100g smoked bacon, diced

2 large onions, sliced

1 tbsp vegetable oil

2 bay leaves

2 sprigs of thyme

10 mushrooms, sliced

1 stick of celery, finely chopped

3 carrots, peeled and diced

3 banana shallots, roughly sliced

200ml red wine

300ml chicken stock

¼ tsp ground cinnamon

¼ tsp ground nutmeg

¼ tsp ground ginger

150-200g gravy granules

500g shortcrust pastry

1 egg, beaten

Pinch of sea salt

Preheat the oven to 180°c.

Heat a large pan and fry off the meat in batches until evenly coloured. Remove all the meat from the pan and fry the bacon and onions in the vegetable oil until slightly golden.

Transfer all the meat back to the pan and add the bay leaves, thyme, mushrooms, celery, carrots and shallots. Coat all the meat and allow it to cook for a few minutes before adding the red wine and chicken stock. Bring to the boil, turn down the heat and allow to cook for 1 hour and 15 minutes.

When the filling is cooked through, season it with the cinnamon, nutmeg and ginger. Thicken with gravy granules to desired consistency.

Roll out the pastry to cover a 24cm non-stick ovenproof dish and make a lid for the pie. Line the dish with the pastry base, fill it with the pie mix and then top with the lid. Trim off the excess pastry and crimp the edges with a fork to seal the lid on. Brush the top with beaten egg to glaze and sprinkle with salt, then bake the pie in the oven for 30 to 40 minutes, or until golden brown.

Preparation time: 20-30 minutes | Cooking time: 1½-2 hours | Serves: 6

DINNER AND A SHOW

THE VILLAGE PUB, RESTAURANT AND LUXURY ACCOMMODATION FOCUSES ON FOOD MADE WITH PEAK LOCAL PRODUCE, ALONGSIDE ELABORATE COCKTAILS AND YORKSHIRE ALES.

Set in the beautiful village of Scalby, near Scarborough, The Plough Inn combines the warm welcome of a Yorkshire pub with award-winning locally-sourced food, drinks and boutique AA 5-Star accommodation, offering visitors a truly unique experience.

Part of the HQ Collection (an eclectic mix of pubs, restaurants and accommodation venues in and around Scalby and Seamer) The Plough is the perfect destination for weekend breakers and holidaymakers keen to sample the very best that the area has to offer.

With an excellent regional reputation already firmly established, The Plough is well on the way to achieving national recognition with an enviable but well-deserved listing in the 2020 Good Food Guide. And it's no surprise as the menu is filled with tempting and delicious dishes prepared with skill and panache.

Head chef Jon Smith takes a seasonal approach in the kitchen; sourcing all produce locally to ensure dishes are prepared and served at their absolute peak. Meat is supplied by Stepney Hill Farm just three miles from the door. The Scarborough Lobster Company ensures a regular supply of delicious, fresh seafood straight from the Yorkshire coast, and with frequent doorstep deliveries from local gamekeepers, it's clear that the provenance and quality of the local ingredients is absolutely central to The Plough's success.

The Yorkshire pride doesn't stop there. The Plough's drinks menu is packed with quality hand-pulled ales from regional breweries which change regularly, plus a growing selection of local spirits including Whitby, Slingsby, Whittaker's and Wild Ram Gin, all born in the rolling hills of Yorkshire.

If cocktails are more your thing, then expect a degree of theatricality in the presentation. Owner Nick Thomas MBE (a Scalby resident for more than 30 years) is also the world's biggest pantomime producer. With hundreds of productions and a coveted Olivier Award under his belt for his shows at the London Palladium, it's only natural that there's an element of surprise, delight and performance in the service! For five star food, drink and accommodation look no further than The Plough.

ALE BRAISED BEEF SHORT RIB, SPELT AND SAGE PESTO

"For me, this dish sums up The Plough: it's about warmth, comfort and generosity…with a bit of a twist! This cut of beef requires a long slow cook to release its wonderful flavour and texture. Makes me proper chuffed to be a Yorkshireman!" Recipe by head chef Jon Smith.

FOR THE BEEF

4 beef short ribs (sometimes known as Jacob's ladder)

2 large shallots, peeled and halved

3 cloves of garlic, crushed

2 carrots, roughly chopped

2 sticks of celery, roughly chopped

Sprig of thyme

2 bay leaves

4 star anise

500ml dark ale (we would use Wold Top Marmalade Porter)

500ml beef stock

2 tbsp honey

1 tbsp tomato purée

FOR THE PESTO

Large bunch of sage, leaves only

4 cloves of garlic, peeled

100g hard cheese, grated

50g hazelnuts, roasted

100ml rapeseed oil

FOR THE SPELT

100g pearled spelt

Chopped flat parsley

50g cold butter, cubed

FOR THE BEEF

Season the short ribs then sear them in a preheated ovenproof pan until very brown all over. Turn down the heat, remove the ribs and pour off any excess fat.

Gently cook the shallots, garlic, carrots and celery in the pan until soft. Add the thyme, bay leaves, anise, beer, beef stock, honey and tomato purée. Stir to combine everything then gently return the short ribs to the pan, cover with the lid and cook in a preheated oven at 160°c for 4 hours and 30 minutes, or until the beef is meltingly tender.

FOR THE PESTO

Add all the ingredients to a food processor and pulse until quite smooth, then season to taste.

FOR THE SPELT

About 40 minutes before the beef is ready, bring 600ml of salted water to the boil in a large saucepan. Add the pearled spelt, simmer for 30 to 40 minutes until the grain is soft but still retains a bit of a bite, then drain off any excess water.

TO SERVE

Remove the beef from the oven and skim off any fat that has risen to the surface. Add two or three spoonfuls of the braising liquid to the spelt then gently stir in the parsley and cold butter until smooth and creamy. Check the seasoning and add salt if needed.

Remove the short ribs from the pan, then strain and reserve the remaining braising liquid. Place a spoonful of spelt in each bowl and place a beef rib on top. Drizzle over the braising liquor and dollop the pesto around. Serve with root vegetables such as carrots, turnips, swede and celeriac.

Preparation time: 30 minutes | Cooking time: 5 hours (but it's worth the wait!) | Serves: 4

GETTING
BACK TO
OUR ROOTS

BRINGING THE FARM TO THE CITY, ROOTS YORK IS A RESTAURANT STEEPED IN TOMMY BANKS' UNIQUE APPROACH TO SEASONALITY AND A RESPONSE TO THE CHALLENGE OF WORKING WITH HOME-GROWN PRODUCE ALL YEAR ROUND.

The seeds of an idea that became Roots York grew, rather appropriately, on the family farm in Oldstead. Tommy, James, Anne and Tom Banks run The Black Swan there – a Michelin-starred restaurant on the edge of the North Yorkshire moors – which has its own two acre kitchen garden. This was so productive that it became apparent there was food to spare, so they joined forces with good friend and business partner Matthew Lockwood to create a second outlet. They wanted Roots to be very different from the world-renowned Black Swan, and so rather than creating a tasting menu, small plates were devised around the available produce to be enjoyed separately or as part of a feast chosen by the chefs.

The new venture took root in a former pub, slightly off the beaten track but just a couple of minutes from the centre of York. Tommy describes the concept as "taking a bit of Oldstead to the city" which is evident everywhere, even in the décor of the beautiful old building. All the tables, for example, are made individually at the workshop on the farm, and have root-like ironwork reaching down the legs, a visible expression of the connection Roots is establishing with York. There's also handmade pottery produced by an artist in the city which Tommy calls 'functional art' – a marriage between traditional materials and quality without pretension, which is central to the whole ethos.

Shared understanding – between nature and food, seasons and produce, Roots and The Black Swan at Oldstead – has also been a key feature of the restaurant since its conception. All the staff, a team of around 40 people including head chef Sean Wrest and restaurant manager Emma Byrne, were trained in Oldstead so that skills and knowledge could be carried over. Three chefs work full time on the farm to preserve produce for the leaner times of year, which is all taken carefully into consideration by Tommy's approach to seasonal cooking.

"Traditional seasons don't actually have much relevance to what we are cooking and growing on the farm," Tommy explains, "and from my perspective there are only three." The first six months of the calendar year rely heavily on stored produce during 'the hunger gap' which is followed by 'the time of abundance' between June and September, and then the preservation season which ekes out the last of the harvest. The menu at Roots does change more than three times a year, reacting to the best times to use all the produce on the farm, embracing nature and chefs' creativity to put harmonious combinations on the plate and celebrate the roots of what we eat.

OATS, BERRIES AND TARRAGON

*Oats, Berries and Tarragon is a dessert served during our 'Time of Abundance' season
at Roots, using fruits and berries picked daily from our garden at Oldstead. We create a
delicious oat mousse then add layers of strawberry jelly and berries macerated in tarragon
sugar, finished with tarragon meringues and strawberry sherbet.*

FOR THE OAT MOUSSE

35g porridge oats

350ml double cream

3g gelatine leaf

200g condensed milk

FOR THE STRAWBERRY JELLY

200g strawberries

30g water

3g gelatine leaf

15g sugar

FOR THE TARRAGON SUGAR

110g sugar

11g fresh tarragon

**FOR THE TARRAGON
MERINGUE**

50g egg whites

1g cream of tartar

100g tarragon sugar

**FOR THE STRAWBERRY
SHERBET**

5ml strawberry juice

50g caster sugar

2g citric acid

TO GARNISH

*400g berries (a selection of seasonal
berries which could include strawberries,
raspberries, blackberries gooseberries and
blueberries)*

FOR THE OAT MOUSSE

Toast the oats in the oven at 180°c for 25 minutes, then stir them into the cream, cover with cling film and leave for 12 hours. Pour the infused cream through a fine sieve. Put the gelatine in cold water for 5 minutes then gently squeeze out the excess water. Warm 50ml of the oat cream in a pan, then add the gelatine and stir until dissolved. Mix in the condensed milk. In a separate bowl, whip the remaining oat cream, then fold the warm mixture into it. Leave to set in the fridge for 12 hours, then lightly beat until smooth before serving.

FOR THE STRAWBERRY JELLY

Bring a pan of water to the boil while you quarter the strawberries. Place them in a bowl with the water, cover tightly with cling film and place over the pan to cook until pale. Strain the cooked strawberries through a sieve to collect the juices. Keep 5ml aside for the strawberry sherbet.

Put the gelatine in cold water for 5 minutes then gently squeeze out the excess water. Mix the sugar with the strawberry juice until dissolved, then the same with the gelatine. Leave the jelly in the fridge for 12 hours to set.

FOR THE TARRAGON SUGAR

Blend the sugar and tarragon together until smooth, then spread the mixture out on a tray. Leave to dry at room temperature for 12 hours, then crush to remove any lumps. Set 10g aside for the berries.

FOR THE TARRAGON MERINGUE

Whisk the egg whites and cream of tartar together until the mixture becomes fluffy. Add the tarragon sugar one tablespoon at a time and continue whisking until stiff, smooth and glossy. Pipe small droplets of the mixture onto a lined baking tray, then bake the meringues at 90°c for 2 hours and 30 minutes.

FOR THE STRAWBERRY SHERBET

Mix all the ingredients together until smooth, spread out on a tray to dry at room temperature for 12 hours, then blend the sherbet into a powder.

TO SERVE

Mix the fresh berries with the 10g of tarragon sugar and leave them to macerate for 15 minutes before beginning to plate the dessert. Pipe a ring of oat mousse around each of the serving plates, then spoon jelly into the centre and top with macerated berries. Finish with a few meringue droplets and a sprinkle of strawberry sherbet.

Preparation time: 2 hours, plus 24 hours infusing and setting | Baking time: 2 hours 30 minutes | Serves: 8

FUSION FLAVOURS

TAKEN FROM THE JAPANESE WORD SUKOSHI, MEANING 'A LITTLE', SKOSH IS A CONTEMPORARY DINING CONCEPT WHERE DINERS ENJOY SMALL PLATES OF ECLECTIC DISHES INSPIRED BY ASIAN FLAVOURS.

Skosh was opened by chef-owner Neil Bentinck in June 2016, inspired by many years as a chef and his travels around the world. Neil grew up surrounded by a love of food, particularly thanks to the culinary heritage of his Indian father. However it wasn't until he was an adult that his passion for food really took hold.

Neil worked in Australia and travelled around much of South-east Asia, eating his way around Thailand, Japan and Singapore, sampling myriad dishes and making notes of his favourite flavour combinations.

As well as his travels, it was living in Australia that opened his eyes to the incredible world of Asian food. With such a rich tapestry of cultures intertwined in the Aussie food scene, the country has absorbed culinary inspiration from across Asia. Being immersed into this exciting melting pot of flavours inspired in Neil a whole new approach to cooking.

Back in the UK, Neil worked as a chef at various restaurants, before becoming head chef at Van Zeller in Harrogate. When he left Van Zeller, he knew that he wanted to do his own thing. It was a couple of years in the making from that point, but in June 2016, Skosh opened its doors just beyond the Micklegate bar in York.

The menu is an intriguing selection of small plates that take inspiration from the fresh, spicy and aromatic flavours of Asia, combining them with local ingredients, too. Think Whitby lobster dumplings with pickled ginger or Lindisfarne oyster with nori vodka and yuzu granita.

It's a flexible dining experience where the staff tailor the experience to the needs of each table. Some people like to graze as they go, ordering a few plates at a time to share amongst the group. Others prefer a more formal experience, being served course by course. Either way is fine – or anything in-between.

Despite its informal and relaxed atmosphere, Skosh boasts a coveted Michelin Bib Gourmand – the only one in York, and one of only three in all of Yorkshire. Bib Gourmands highlight quality cooking at accessible prices – and this, in essence, is what Skosh is all about.

PORK BELLY 'MASSAMAN' WITH APPLE AND PEANUT

A massaman curry is a wonderful thing… hailing from Thailand yet heady with spices often associated with Indian cuisine. At Skosh, the dish is slightly refined, separating the meat from the sauce, yet taste-wise, still in keeping with the original. At the restaurant, we brine the meat for several hours and slowly steam overnight, however this does not have to be the case at home!

FOR THE PORK BELLY

2k pork belly, skinless and boneless
2 tsp salt and 2 tsp sugar
50g vegetable oil

FOR THE CURRY PASTE

250ml vegetable oil
50g dried red chillies
4 large banana shallots, sliced
35g garlic, crushed
100g ginger, sliced
50g lemongrass, chopped
1 tbsp ground coriander
2 tsp each ground cloves, cumin, cinnamon and nutmeg
1 tsp each ground anise, turmeric & salt

FOR THE CURRY SAUCE

200g shallots, sliced
600ml beef stock
50ml fish sauce
125g tamarind concentrate
100g light soft brown sugar
100ml coconut milk
400g tin coconut cream

FOR THE CRISPY POTATOES

2 large chipping potatoes eg. Maris Piper
Vegetable oil, for frying and salt

TO SERVE

Maldon sea salt flakes
Chilli oil, to drizzle
Roasted salted peanuts, coarsely chopped
1 Granny Smith apple, cut into julienne

FOR THE PORK BELLY

Preheat the oven to 140°c. Season the pork all over with salt and sugar and rub with oil to coat. Sit the pork on a rack over a deep baking tray. Cover with a sheet of greaseproof paper and plenty of foil. Add 500ml water to the tray, then tightly wrap the tray in foil. Place in the oven and cook slowly for 4 hours, until tender when pierced with a sharp knife. Allow to cool slightly, then wrap in cling film. Place the pork on a plate, fat-side down, then place a tray on top and weigh down. (The pork is pressing to set the shape for later on – too heavy a weight and too much juice will be lost.) Chill overnight, then cut into rectangles, then across into slices.

FOR THE MASSAMAN CURRY PASTE

Heat the oil slowly in a deep pot, then add all the ingredients. Bring to the boil, then turn the heat down to a simmer for 15 minutes. Allow to cool slightly, then blend to a smooth paste. Store in the fridge until required. (This makes more than required but will keep for months in the fridge.)

FOR THE CURRY SAUCE

Sauté the shallots in a touch of oil until soft, then add 150g of the curry paste and stir fry to release the aromas. Add all the other ingredients with a little salt and bring to the boil, then reduce to a steady simmer for 30 minutes. Blend with a hand blender, then thicken with a little cornflour if required and pass through a sieve. Taste it. The sauce should be sweet and sour with salt and spice. At this point, season to balance the flavours with lime juice/tamarind/salt/fish sauce and sugar.

FOR THE CRISPY POTATOES

Slice the potatoes very thinly on a mandoline fitted with the medium toothed blade. Alternatively slice as finely as possible in long slices then go back across with a knife – you want very fine shreds or 'julienne'. Soak the potatoes in water and agitate to release the starch. Drain and dry on kitchen towel. Heat the oil to 160°c and add the potatoes, being careful as they may spit. Allow to crisp in the oil – when the bubbles disappear and they are lightly browned it's a good indication they are crisp. Drain on kitchen paper and season with salt.

TO SERVE

Heat some curry sauce in a pan and keep warm. Fry the pork slices in a light film of vegetable oil in a large non-stick frying pan, then drain and season with salt flakes. Place the pork slices in a bowl and pour the sauce around. Drizzle with chilli oil and sprinkle over some peanuts. Neatly arrange a stack of apple strips and some crispy potatoes alongside. Enjoy!

Preparation time: 1 hour, plus overnight chilling the pork | Cooking time: 4 hours | Serves 4

WHISKY BUSINESS

WITH FILEY BAY – YORKSHIRE'S FIRST EVER SINGLE MALT – LAUNCHED ON THE 5TH OCTOBER 2019, THE SPIRIT OF YORKSHIRE DISTILLERY IS MAKING WAVES IN THE WORLD OF WHISKY WITH ITS UNIQUE 'FIELD TO BOTTLE' PROCESS.

The idea for The Spirit of Yorkshire Distillery came into being in 2012 and work began behind the scenes to establish the distillery, with the first distillations in 2016. Using stills from Forsyths and barley from its own farm on the Yorkshire Wolds, Spirit of Yorkshire is able to have a little more flexibility than a Scotch distillery, allowing the team to introduce a column still, for example. This is just one of the ways in which the daring new venture tries hard to learn the processes of whisky and reinvent them without being anarchic, resulting in something wonderfully unique.

The single malt whisky – which is creamy, light and fruity with flavours of vanilla, honey, citrus and caramel – is named Filey Bay, paying homage to the team's love of the North Yorkshire Coast. "We're really proud of our local area and love where we're from." They refer to the whisky as not just made in but made of Yorkshire; from employing local people to using the farm's own water supply, it's a home-grown product through and through. Founders Tom and David are old friends whose idea for Spirit of Yorkshire Distillery developed out of their knowledge in farming and crop science respectively. Tom is a third generation farmer on whose farm all the barley used in

the distillery is grown, using progressive methods to protect soil structure for future harvests. The Yorkshire Wolds are well known for malting barley, the majority of which is transported up to Scotland, so part of the drive was to make use of that resource within the region that it's grown.

There's more to the distillery than Yorkshire's first single malt whisky though, as the team have been busy running daily tours (which are Visit England Quality Assured), as well as The Pot Still Coffee Shop. As the name suggests, this relaxed space offers views of the whisky stills along with homemade cakes, lunches and breakfasts made with locally sourced produce wherever possible. It's also a finalist for Deliciously Yorkshire's Best Afternoon Tea Award 2019. Music nights featuring local artists make the distillery even more of a destination, marking it out as somewhere that respects tradition but does things its own way. The future looks very bright for Spirit of Yorkshire Distillery, full of excitement for where its unique approach will go next, and bursting with pride for the land that made this innovation possible.

FILEY BAY ESPRESSO MARTINI AND MACARONS

*Our co-founder David is a macaron whizz, and coffee shop manager Serena loves
an Espresso Martini. How could we make them even better? Introduce Filey Bay
Yorkshire Single Malt into them, of course, for a delicious after-dark treat.*

FOR THE MACARONS

100g ground almonds

100g icing sugar

90g egg white

Pinch of salt

135g caster sugar

40ml water

2 tsp pink food colouring

FOR THE FILLING

200g white chocolate

10 fl oz (285ml) whisky

66g double cream

½ tsp orange blossom water

Fresh raspberries, to decorate

FOR THE ESPRESSO MARTINI

100g caster sugar

50ml water

100ml Filey Bay Single Malt Whisky

50ml espresso

50ml coffee liqueur

Coffee beans, to decorate

FOR THE MACARONS

Preheat the oven to 160°c and line a baking sheet with a non-slip mat or parchment paper. Blitz the almonds and icing sugar in a food processor until fine, then sieve twice. Briefly beat 70g of the egg white with the salt in an electric mixer. Put the caster sugar and water in a small pan and mix well, then heat to 118-120°c. When the sugar reaches 115°c start to whisk the egg whites on a medium speed. When they are foamy and the sugar syrup is 118-120°c, carefully pour the syrup into the egg whites in a thin stream towards the side of the bowl while whisking on a medium speed. Once all of the sugar syrup is added, turn the speed up and whisk until very stiff and glossy, and the mixture has cooled to room temperature.

Fold in the ground almonds and icing sugar along with the remaining egg white, then beat the mixture just until smooth and fairly thick, but not so thick that it doesn't move. You should be able to draw a figure of eight with the batter, which holds a visible shape for about 3 seconds. Colour the batter lightly with the pink food colouring.

Put an 8mm nozzle into a piping bag and paint pink food colouring in stripes on the inside of the bag. Load the macaron mixture into the bag, and pipe blobs of batter no bigger than a 10p onto the baking sheet. Drop the tray gently onto the worktop to get rid of any air bubbles. Place the tray into the oven and immediately turn it down to 160°c (without the fan if possible). Bake for 7½ minutes, then move down to middle shelf and bake for a further 7½ minutes. Remove and leave to cool, while you repeat the process with the remaining batter.

FOR THE FILLING

Melt the white chocolate in a bain-marie, then whisk in the Filey Bay, double cream and orange blossom water. When the macarons are cool to the touch, use about one teaspoon of cream filling to stick them together in pairs. Serve them with fresh raspberries alongside the martini.

FOR THE ESPRESSO MARTINI

To make the sugar syrup, pour the caster sugar and water into a small pan on a medium heat. Stir, bring to the boil then turn off the heat and leave to cool. Place a handful of ice in the shaker with the Filey Bay Single Malt, espresso, coffee liqueur and sugar syrup. Shake then serve in a chilled glass, decorated with the coffee beans.

Preparation time: 30 minutes | Cooking time: 30 minutes | Makes: 15 macarons and 1 martini

YORKSHIRE
BAKED AND BREWED

VALE OF MOWBRAY HAVING BEEN BREWING AND BAKING SINCE THE 18TH CENTURY, PERFECTING THE PORK PIES THAT ARE PROUDLY YORKSHIRE (AND NOTHING TO DO WITH THOSE OTHER PORK PIES THAT SHARE THE NAME!)

In 1795 Vale of Mowbray opened as a brewery and turned out proper Yorkshire beer until 1928, when it became a bakery under the same name. 2018 marked 90 years of making pork pies, which are still produced in very traditional ways. Some of the machinery has been around for more than 50 years and still going strong! The basic recipe hasn't been tinkered with either, although progress has been marked by the construction of a brand new bakery in 2003, the introduction of several new and daring twists on the classic pork pie, and of course the ever-growing sales which have surpassed two million per week thanks to their enduring popularity.

Alongside pies in different sizes and rectangular 'County' and 'Grosvenor' pies, which include boiled eggs, Vale of Mowbray has embraced a match made in heaven for one of its newest creations: a cheese and pickle pork pie. The company also partnered with local producer Calder's Kitchen, a very small operation supplying delicious piccalilli to the pie giants. The piccalilli and spicy piccalilli pies use an entry-level variety and another named 'Sillylilli' in reference to its chilli heat, for the adventurous… All Vale of Mowbray pork pies are filled with cured meat and encased in classic hot water pastry, but the unique blend of herbs and spices are a well-kept secret!

Judges at the Great British Food Awards 2019 have had their turn at uncovering these mysteries; two varieties were sent off to Monica Galetti and Glynn Purnell and received Highly Commended from the judges. The Piccalilli Pork Pie has also been shortlisted for the best in its category at the Deliciouslyorkshire Taste Awards. Everything from curing the pork to packaging the finished product is done in-house at the factory, which sits as it always has on the strip of land between the North Yorkshire moors and the Dales. "We've stuck to our guns, continued to make what we know, and it's done us right," says Jason, who has been part of developments to keep the company moving forwards with integrity.

Despite immense pride in this regional heritage and identity, Vale of Mowbray is something of a mystery to the locals – except the many who work there – and so the company is keen to showcase its pies and Yorkshire pride at shows and events across the county. The team also look forward to meeting more local suppliers like Calder's Kitchen, and have plenty more inventions in the pipeline for their pies in the near future.

SWEET CHILLI GARLIC SAUCE WITH ZESTY ONIONS

We know that people love dipping our pies in a tasty sauce or chutney. Well, this is something we also like doing, and our bakery is chock full of different condiments that we've tested with our pies, so we thought it would be nice to share one of the creations we love here at Vale of Mowbray.

FOR THE CHILLI SAUCE

300g fresh chillies (about 12 chillies, mixed varieties or use your favourite)

4 cloves of garlic

100ml maple syrup

100ml water

25ml mirin (Japanese sweet rice wine)

25ml light soy sauce

1 tbsp cider vinegar

FOR THE ZESTY ONIONS

4 shallots

1 tsp rapeseed oil

1 lime, juiced

Salt and pepper

FOR THE CHILLI SAUCE

Remove the stalks and roughly chop the chillies. Leave the seeds in unless the variety of chillies you are using is extremely hot; you may want to remove seeds from these ones. Give the garlic a rough chop and bruise to release the flavour.

Add all the ingredients to a pan and bring to the boil. Lower the heat and simmer for 10 to 15 minutes, stirring to ensure it doesn't catch and burn. Blend the sauce and reduce it to your desired consistency. Once cooled, serve or store in an airtight container.

FOR THE ZESTY ONIONS

Peel and slice the shallots while you heat a pan to medium. Add the oil and shallots to the pan, cook until almost caramelised while stirring, then add the lime juice. Season to taste with salt and pepper and stir well to make sure all the flavours are combined. Once cool, store in an airtight container.

TO SERVE

Take the lid off your favourite Vale of Mowbray pie, spoon on some onions and drizzle over however much chilli sauce you like. Pop the lid on top, maybe at a jaunty angle because that's kind of cute, then tuck in!

Preparation time: 5 minutes | Cooking time: 15 minutes | Serves: 10

THE CITY WITH TASTE

DISCOVER THE DESTINATION FOR FOODIES AND THOSE LOOKING FOR A SPECIAL CULINARY EXPERIENCE, WITH A VAST RANGE OF DELICIOUS DISHES WAITING TO BE DISCOVERED.

York hosts everything from fine dining to international street food; there really is something for every palate. Treat yourself to a sharing plate experience at Roots York, the brainchild of celebrity chef Tommy Banks, where you can sample dishes from their tasting menu, made up of the best locally sourced produce: every spoonful is a taste of Yorkshire. The Ivy St Helen's Square offers a contemporary British menu in sophisticated, beautifully decorated surroundings.

For something relaxing, stop by Pairings Wine Bar where they'll match some of the best regional food dishes with the best wines and ales, in tranquil surroundings. Michelin-starred chef Andrew Pern's two restaurants offer different experiences. Mr P's Curious Tavern offers a quirky spin on traditional pub grub, while The Star Inn The City serves a variety of starters, mains and puddings on the banks of the River Ouse. Dip into the many quirky coffee and tea shops that line the cobbled streets of York, serving a huge range of hot drinks and delicious cakes, from the quaint Crumbs Cupcakery to the cosy Brew and Brownie.

The city not only boasts regional cuisine but showcases a wide range of global food. Fancy Hank's Bar and Kitchen brings good old fashioned American flavours from the Deep South to North Yorkshire. Experience continental al fresco Italian dining at Lucia Wine Bar and Grill, or visit family-run restaurant Barbakan for hearty servings of traditional Polish food.

Just a short stroll from Europe's oldest medieval street is the Shambles Food Court. Open all year round, there is huge variety of street food delights waiting to be tucked into. Don't miss Los Moros, where you can satisfy those cravings with fabulous North African and Middle Eastern style street food. Due to huge demand, Los Moros have also opened up their own restaurant on the neighbouring Grape Lane. Other street food outlets include healthy fast food from KREP in the form of crêpes and galettes, pizza treats from Pizzoli and scrummy sausages from Shambles Kitchen.

Every September, the York Food and Drink Festival fills the streets with delicious sights, smells and tastes for a full week. You'll also have the opportunity to learn some culinary skills at the cooking classes and chef demonstrations led by celebrity and regional chefs.

Cafés, restaurants, street food stalls, taverns, inns and festivals abound in York: whichever corner you turn, new culinary discoveries await and will leave you in no doubt that this is a city with taste!

IMMERSIVE
CULINARY
EXPERIENCES

NOT ONLY CAN YOU DEVOUR AND ENJOY TASTY TREATS IN YORK, YOU CAN ALSO DISCOVER UNIQUE IMMERSIVE EXPERIENCES, PERFECT FOR ANYONE INTERESTED IN FOOD AND DRINK.

York is the home of chocolate. You've heard of the iconic KitKat and Terry's Chocolate Orange, but did you know these creations were crafted in York? Find out more about the city's rich chocolate heritage at York's Chocolate Story, where you can also get hands on and create your own chocolate lolly. After you've taken the tour, explore the Chocolate Trail, where you can see the original site of the first Rowntree's chocolate shop and visit Goddards House and Garden, the former home of chocolatier Noel Terry.

After a busy morning of exploration, sit back, relax and enjoy some chit chat over an afternoon tea. The world famous Bettys is arguably the pioneer of the afternoon tea experience, and is a must see thanks to decadent interiors, mouth-watering cakes and refreshing teas. Alternatively, visit the Countess of York, where you'll enjoy afternoon tea aboard a beautifully restored train carriage.

A recent addition to the city's street food scene is Brew York's brand new Beer Hall. This city centre craft brewery originally opened in August 2016 with a riverside tap room attached. However, in the summer of 2018 the brewery expanded into the neighbouring building and opened the Beer Hall. The venue serves 40 beers at a time to suit all tastes, but look out for more unusual flavours including Rhubarbra Streisand, a rhubarb and custard flavoured pale ale. And what better food to accompany a beer than a burger? Born To Lose can make this dream pairing a reality, as well as offering Asian inspired fusion food, within the Beer Hall.

If you think you're the master chef or best baker in your household, roll up your sleeves and put your skills to the test at The Cookery School, located at The Grand Hotel. Here, professional chefs will enhance your cookery skills, covering everything from bread making to Indian cuisine.

Lastly, take home a little piece of York by visiting some of the best specialist and artisan food shops within the city walls. Love Cheese is home to over 100 different cheeses from across Yorkshire and the globe. The popular York Gin is the only gin produced in the city, and the full award-winning range is stocked in the distillery's very own shop near the Shambles.

With so much to discover in York, you'll be coming back for seconds!

www.visityork.org/eat-and-drink

ICONIC
YORKSHIRE WENSLEYDALE

SET IN THE HEART OF THE YORKSHIRE DALES IS THE WENSLEYDALE CREAMERY, HOME OF YORKSHIRE WENSLEYDALE CHEESE AND ITS FANTASTIC VISITOR CENTRE.

The Wensleydale Creamery is an award-winning, independent, traditional cheese-maker and specialist blender of cheese with ingredients. They use traditional methods to handcraft cheese to time-honoured recipes, using milk from local farms, as well as being innovative with the development of new cheese recipes. Steeped in heritage and provenance, they are custodians of tradition with a 1000-year history, relevant to the 21st century.

Producing approximately 4000 tonnes of cheese, and operating one of the top tourist destinations in the Yorkshire Dales, they are truly a community-based business, being a major provider of rural jobs, contributing £13m to the local economy annually.

Their range of artisan cheeses are handcrafted by a team of devoted master cheese-makers. From Yorkshire Wensleydale to Wensleydale Blue and Kit Calvert Old-style Wensleydale, the cheeses are matured under the watchful eye of a specialist cheese-grader.

Yorkshire Wensleydale cheese is world-famous. In December 2013, it achieved European Protected Geographical Indication Status (PGI). Wensleydale cheese can be made anywhere. Only Yorkshire Wensleydale is handcrafted by skilled cheese-makers to a time-honoured recipe in the designated area of

Wensleydale, in the heart of the Yorkshire Dales National Park, using milk from local farms, and their own unique cheese-making starter cultures.

So what is the secret to the popularity of this classic cheese? A distinctive crumbly texture, steeped in history and years of knowledge, skill and craftsmanship, passed down through generations of expert cheese-makers that is now widely celebrated.

Whether taking in pride of place on a cheeseboard or sliced on top of fruitcake, this much-loved cheese has been enjoyed for generations. However, it's within some of the country's favourite dishes where the crumbly texture and creamy taste of Yorkshire Wensleydale really speaks for itself.

Due to its unique structure, Yorkshire Wensleydale doesn't melt like other cheese when cooked, it retains its wonderful texture and flavour. That's why this iconic cheese lends itself so nicely to adding that special touch to recipes – crumbled into a warm summer greens salad and enjoyed in the garden, or crumbled onto a delicious tart to enjoy next to a roaring fire in the colder months. It really is a cheese that should be in every cook's kitchen.

PIZZA WITH PARMA HAM, AVOCADO AND YORKSHIRE WENSLEYDALE CHEESE

Make pizza night even more special with a crumble of Yorkshire Wensleydale! You can use a shop-bought pizza base for this deliciously different pizza – or if you've got time, make the pizza dough using the recipe here.

100g Yorkshire Wensleydale cheese

1 garlic clove

1 red onion

Olive oil, for cooking

2 pizza bases (shop-bought or homemade, see recipe below)

6 tbsp passata tomato sauce

1 ripe avocado

10 slices Parma ham

2 sprigs of fresh basil, leaves ripped

TO MAKE PIZZA DOUGH

250g bread flour

1 tsp Maldon sea salt flakes

2 tbsp olive oil

1 sachet fast-action yeast

160ml warm water

Semolina flour, for dusting

Preheat the oven to 220°c. Finely chop the garlic and half of the red onion. Fry the garlic and chopped red onion in a pan with a little olive oil until soft. Add the passata and heat through.

Place three tablespoons of the tomato sauce onto each pizza base and spread outwardly until each base is covered with a fine layer of sauce.

Thinly slice the other half of the red onion and the avocado, then place the slices on top of the pizza. Top with ripped basil leaves. Remove the fat from the Parma ham, rip into pieces and place on top of the pizza base. Crumble the Yorkshire Wensleydale cheese on top, (remember to save some for the next step!), ensuring it goes right to the edges, and bake in the preheated oven until the crust is golden brown.

Finally, for added specialness, crumble a tiny bit more Yorkshire Wensleydale cheese on top before serving.

TO MAKE PIZZA DOUGH

If you are making your own pizza dough… Sift the flour into a bowl, add the salt flakes and stir. Place the rest of the ingredients in the warm water and stir well. Pour the warm water mix into the flour and mix well until it forms a dough. Place onto a surface, lightly floured with semolina flour. Knead together for 8 minutes by hand or 5 minutes in a food mixer. Place in a bowl, cover with a damp cloth, then allow to prove in a warm place for 1 to 1½ hours until risen. Once lightly risen, place onto a lightly floured board and cut into portions. Roll into balls and press in the centre. Then pick up the dough and press into a thin pizza shape encouraging the main part of the dough to the edges.

Preparation time: 15 minutes, plus 1½ hours if making dough | Cooking time: 15 minutes | Serves 2

A PERFECT MATCH

FROM THE FIRST COMMISSION IN 2014 TO CREATING OVER A HUNDRED CAKES IN 2019, WEDDING SPECIALIST WHERE THE RIBBON ENDS HAS FLOURISHED AT ITS FAMILY HOME, JERVAULX ABBEY TEAROOM.

Gayle Hussan grew up around cakes at her family's tearoom in the Yorkshire Dales, but never imagined one day establishing a business that would create beautiful wedding centrepieces. She took a course in finishing fruitcakes, which covered marzipan and icing with sugar flowers, and the elegant decorations immediately sparked her interest. Gayle continued to teach herself the art of sugarcraft and absolutely fell in love with the process, developing a style of her own through making cakes for friend's birthdays until her first wedding commission in 2014.

At that point, her fledging business moved into its permanent home at Jervaulx Abbey Tearoom where Gayle also worked with her mum Carol and sister Anna for a while. Things really took off for Where The Ribbon Ends after word of mouth brought in more and more enquiries, and gradually involved the whole family. Anna began to experiment with edible painting on the iced cakes which she quickly developed a real talent for, and Carol has passed on years of baking knowledge to both her daughters, so every cake they make is truly a team effort.

Gayle knew from the beginning that she wanted to create pretty yet modern cakes with a big emphasis on attention to detail, which is referenced in the name: they will always place something over the ribbon ends so that the back of the cake looks as finished and beautiful as the front. Of course, it also has to taste great! Where The Ribbon Ends has a 'menu' of around 30 flavours to choose from at consultations, but the end result is always completely bespoke and personalised for the couple and their day. Gayle even takes inspiration from colour schemes, dresses, flower arrangements and other details to produce the cake of their dreams!

This dedication to quality and design as well as taste has recently won the small team a big accolade, in the form of a national award. After being voted the North East and Yorkshire winner by customers, a panel of experts from The Wedding Industry recognised a champion in Where The Ribbon Ends. Things keep moving onwards and upwards for the family venture, with a studio now located in the tearoom for consultations, beautiful displays and, most recently, hosting small classes to share their handcrafting and home baking skills. "Each year surprises us with what it brings," says Gayle, "but contributing to someone's wedding day is always the best part."

Although wedding cake specialists, overleaf, they share some of their favourite recipes to help you make elements of your own dessert table such as cookies and classic vanilla cupcakes.

Additional photography: Emily Olivia Photography and Jessica J Photography

BE HAPPY EAT CAKE

BESPOKE COOKIES

These buttery beauties are so versatile and perfect for decorating as they don't lose their shape while baking. We top them with a fondant disc, and from there you can personalise the cookie with your own artistic flair. We specialise in our bespoke and hand-painted designs.

230g unsalted butter

175g caster sugar

1 egg

2 tsp vanilla extract

400g plain flour

Preheat the oven to 170°c and make sure the butter is at room temperature. Beat the butter and sugar with an electric mixer on a high speed for a couple of minutes, until the mixture turns pale.

Scrape down the sides of the mixing bowl, then add the egg and vanilla extract. Continue mixing at high speed until the egg is thoroughly incorporated. Reduce the speed and add the plain flour to form fairly dry biscuit dough.

Turn the dough out onto a lightly floured surface (don't use too much flour as this will affect the texture) and roll it out to the desired thickness, we suggest 1cm. Use a 7½cm cutter to create rounds and place them onto a non-stick baking tray. Bake the cookies in the preheated oven for around 7 minutes. Put the timer on after 5 minutes and keep a close eye on the cookies from that point.

Once they are slightly golden, remove them from the oven and set aside to cool for 5 minutes on the tray. Carefully transfer each cookie onto a wire rack to cool completely.

Now you can decorate the cookies however you wish. Melted chocolate, sprinkles, marshmallows and edible decorations are perfect for kids (young and old) to play with. We top them with a fondant disc and then decorate from there. To do this, roll out the fondant – not too thick, but not so thin that it could break – then use the same size cutter that you used for the cookies to cut out rounds. Use an edible 'glue' to attach the fondant to the cookie, such as royal icing. You now have a blank canvas to create anything you wish; use edible paints or decorations to finish…or just eat them! The cookies also freeze well without toppings or decoration.

Preparation time: 10 minutes | Cooking time: 5-7 minutes | Makes: 30

BROWNIE STACKS

*What makes a good brownie? If you immediately think of a gooey centre and a
crisp topping, then this is the recipe for you. The yummiest chocolate brownies on
display almost look too good to eat... almost!*

280g butter

280g dark chocolate

415g sugar

5 eggs

60g cocoa powder, sifted

130g plain flour, sifted

Preheat the oven to 160°c and line a 20 by 20cm tin with baking paper.

Place the chocolate and butter into a bowl over a pan of hot water to melt them, stirring constantly to make sure the chocolate doesn't burn. Set aside to cool.

In a mixing bowl, whisk the sugar and eggs together at high speed until they become paler and thicker. Pour the melted butter and chocolate into the sugar and eggs, while mixing at medium speed until thoroughly combined. Add the cocoa powder and plain flour then mix at low speed until no dry ingredients remain visible.

Pour the mixture into the prepared tin and place into the preheated oven. Bake the brownies for 45 to 55 minutes, using a skewer or thin knife to check them towards the end. A little of the batter will stick but it must be thick and gooey. If not, bake for another few minutes.

Once the brownies are ready, remove the tin from the oven and set aside to cool. Once totally cool, remove the brownies from the tin. Use a sharp knife to create neat edges and mark out a 5 by 5 grid to get approximately 3½ by 3½cm squares, then cut the brownies.

You can now stack your brownies and dress them with fresh fruits, edible flowers, edible dusts or even more chocolate!

Preparation time: 10 minutes | Cooking time: 45-55 minutes | Serves: 25

CLASSIC VANILLA CUPCAKES WITH BUTTERCREAM

Vanilla cupcakes are an absolute classic. They're amazing just as they are, or they can be made as fancy as you like by changing the flavours, decoration or even adding jam into the middle. The buttercream topping turns these humble cupcakes into a stunning creation that can be enjoyed by everyone.

FOR THE CUPCAKES

230g margarine

230g caster sugar

3 eggs

2 tbsp vanilla extract

230g self-raising flour

OPTIONAL

60g cocoa powder

4 lemons, zested

FOR THE BUTTERCREAM

455g butter, at room temperature

455g icing sugar

OPTIONAL

10ml vanilla extract

20ml elderflower cordial

115g cocoa powder

1 tbsp white hot chocolate powder

Preheat the oven to 170°c and place 16 cupcake cases in two 12-hole cupcake tins.

FOR THE CUPCAKES

Cream the margarine and sugar together, beating on a high speed until the mixture is light and fluffy. Scrape down the sides of the bowl as it's beating to make sure it's fully mixed. Add two of the eggs and the vanilla extract on a high speed. Reduce the speed and add a little flour, then slowly increase the speed again and add the last egg and the remaining flour.

Beat for a couple of minutes to ensure everything is thoroughly combined before evenly distributing the mixture into cupcake cases. The amount you put into each case is important; a rounded tablespoon should be perfect. The cupcake case should be half or just below half full. Bake for 20 minutes. The cupcakes should rise to the top of the cases, and you can check they are baked by inserting a skewer, which should come out clean.

To make chocolate cupcakes, swap 60g of flour for the same amount of cocoa powder and don't add any vanilla extract. To make lemon cupcakes, add the zest of four lemons to the mixture. You could even squeeze lemon curd into the centre of the cupcake using a piping bag.

FOR THE BUTTERCREAM

Beat the butter with the icing sugar, starting off slowly to avoid icing sugar flying out, and gaining speed until the mixer is on full power. Then add a splash of liquid, such as water or milk, and beat again until the icing becomes paler in colour. This usually takes 3 to 5 minutes.

You can make various flavours of icing with the optional extras; for vanilla or elderflower icing, add the vanilla extract or cordial at the same point as the liquid. For chocolate icing, add cocoa powder or white hot chocolate powder with the icing sugar. For a dark chocolate flavour, we use Bourneville as it's a beautifully rich cocoa powder. Avoid hot chocolate powders as they are too sweet, but we find Options white hot chocolate powder gives the best white chocolate flavour.

Preparation time: 20 minutes | Cooking time: 20 minutes | Makes: 16

TASTES LIKE HOME

HOME-GROWN, HOME-BAKED AND HOME-COOKED... THE WHOLE HOGG FARM SHOP AND TEAROOM TAKES THE BEST LOCAL PRODUCE AND CELEBRATES ITS UNPARALLELED TASTE.

The Whole Hogg Farm Shop is located on a working farm, a family-run business that decided to diversify some nine years ago. The family team works well, with Chris working the land with their son Tom, while his wife Suzanne co-ordinates the farm shop.

The farm itself produces a variety of crops. Potatoes are one of their biggest crops – a selection of red (Shannon) and white (Estima and Marfona) are available in the farm shop, sold in bags ranging from 5kg to 25kg. Another popular crop is pumpkins. "We are undoubtedly the biggest pumpkin growers in the North," says Suzanne. "Pumpkins are our Christmas!"

The fabulous pumpkins are ready for people to come and enjoy picking every year from early October. Get ready for Halloween by carving your pumpkin, then follow the farm's philosophy of "great taste, less waste" by using the remaining pumpkin to make a delicious soup, like the one overleaf. Sharon, the cook, makes this soup every year, and it's always popular. This year they are also producing pumpkin and ginger jam.

The farm shop also offers beers, wines and spirits, and a range of unusual gifts and gift cards from small producers and local makers.

With an emphasis on home-grown, local produce and great taste, The Whole Hogg Farm Shop offers a friendly and relaxed shopping experience. The well-stocked butchery is the jewel in the crown. The beef sold here isn't just British beef... it's Yorkshire beef! All the meat sold here can be traced back to the field.

The delicatessen offers a tempting selection of scrumptious pies, sausage rolls and quiches, all hand-made on the premises. They also sell their excellent range of ready meals, both main course and puddings, which are available on a weekly basis, made with only the best ingredients.

After completing your shopping, you can relax and unwind in the characterful tearoom. It's the perfect place to sit down with a cup of tea and a freshly baked scone, or to enjoy a full English breakfast, a snack or a hearty meal. Everything is made to order with fresh ingredients, and they try their best to cater for all dietary requirements with a selection of dairy-free and gluten-free cakes available.

Please Do Not Pick
UP PUMPKINS by
there Stalks all
Breakages Must be
Paid for
Thank You

TRICK
or
TREAT

PUMPKIN SOUP

The Whole Hogg is one of the largest pumpkin growers in the North! Pick your own pumpkin then transform it into this warming gluten-free soup. Recipe by Sharon Harland.

2 white onions, peeled and chopped into chunks

2 red onions, peeled and chopped into chunks

4 green peppers, deseeded and chopped into chunks

6 large carrots, peeled and chopped into chunks

2 garlic cloves, peeled

1 medium pumpkin, chopped into chunks (leave the skin on while cooking)

A drizzle of olive oil

A sprinkle of mixed spice

3 gluten-free vegetable stock cubes

1 ½ pints boiling water

Salt and pepper

Single cream, to finish (optional)

Pumpkin seeds, to serve

Preheat the oven to 200°c (gas 6). Put the onions, peppers, carrots, garlic and pumpkin onto a baking tray, coat with a little oil and sprinkle over some mixed spice. Roast in the preheated oven until tender.

Lift the tray out of the oven carefully. Remove the skin from the pumpkin and transfer all the contents of the tray into a large pan.

Place the three vegetable stock cubes into a bowl and add the boiling water. Stir to dissolve the cubes. Add the stock to the soup mix. Bring the soup to the boil and then whizz with a blender until smooth.

Season with salt and pepper and add a little more mixed spice if required. Add a drizzle of cream for added flavour, if you like. Toast some pumpkin seeds and sprinkle on top before serving.

Preparation time: 20 minutes | Cooking time: 1 hour | Serves 12

DISTILLING TRADITION

IN A DISTILLERY IN THE ANCIENT CITY, A GROUP OF GIN-LOVERS ARE PRODUCING THE CITY'S ONLY GINS – AND GATHERING A PLETHORA OF INTERNATIONAL AWARDS FOR THEM, TOO.

Like all good ideas, the initial concept for York Gin was developed in the pub. Current landlord of The Swan Paul Crossman, its former landlord Pete McNichol (who initially established the York Gin Company and now runs sales and distribution), food and drink lover Harry Cooke (who is now chief distiller), and marketer and gin-fan Emma Godivala came together to produce top-quality gins inspired by the city's 2000 years of history.

The first bottles hit the shelves in March 2018, and since then, York Gin quickly established itself in the highly competitive gin world, winning international plaudits and an array of prestigious awards.

The first gin, York Gin London Dry, achieved two stars at the Great Taste Awards 2019. It has a string of awards to its name, thanks to its no-frills, no-gimmicks distillation. Smooth and rounded, this classic London Dry is made with botanicals that were available at the time of the first gin craze in the 18th Century.

York Gin Old Tom launched in summer 2019 and immediately won a Gold Outstanding medal at the International Wine and Spirit Competition, and Gold at the Spirits Business Gin Masters. It's a collaboration with the Michelin-starred Star Inn, Harome, whose chefs created a sugar syrup flavoured with herbs from its own garden and foraged from North Yorkshire hedgerows.

York Gin Outlaw is a 57% Navy Strength Gin, which won Double Gold at the San Francisco World Spirits Competition in 2019. Inspired by York's outlaws, Guy Fawkes, Dick Turpin and 'Yorkshire Witch' Mary Bateman, this is dangerously smooth for its 57% – as it says on the bottle, "serve with ice, tonic ... and care".

York Gin Roman Fruit is a sugar-free, fruit-infused dry gin with a deep red hue, also awarded a Great Taste award. Perfect in summer with a strawberry or raspberry garnish, or at Christmas, accompanied by festive orange peel and cinnamon.

Finally, York Gin Grey Lady, distilled with Earl Grey tea and citrus fruit, then infused with pea flower to give it a ghostly grey-blue hue, is a nod to the Grey Lady, York Theatre Royal's resident ghost. This one hasn't won any awards... for the simple reason that they haven't entered it into any yet.

The distillery in Acaster Malbis runs on 100% green energy. The copper still, Ebor, short for Eboracum (the Roman name for York), runs on green electricity and the finished gins are distilled, bottled and labelled by hand. York Gin is created using the traditional method of vapour distillation, ensuring a very consistent, balanced gin.

The range is available at the York Gin shop, in hundreds of the city's bars, restaurants and pubs, and can even be found as far afield as Scotland and Cornwall.

YORK GIN CLASSIC COCKTAILS

Two classic cocktails are prepared with two of our York Gins here – the Tom Collins featuring our York Gin Old Tom and a Gimlet made with our York Gin London Dry. These are simple, timeless and delicious, letting the taste of the gin take a starring role.

FOR THE YORK GIN TOM COLLINS

50ml York Gin Old Tom

25ml lemon juice

25ml sugar syrup

125ml soda water

Lemon slice, to garnish

Juniper berries, to garnish (optional)

FOR THE YORK GIN GIMLET

50ml York Gin London Dry

30-50ml Rose's Lime Cordial (to taste)

Dash of soda water (optional)

Ice, to serve

Lime slice, to garnish

FOR THE YORK GIN TOM COLLINS

Build the drink over plenty of ice in a tall glass, stir gently and garnish with a slice of lemon and a couple of juniper berries, if you like.

FOR THE YORK GIN GIMLET

Put all the ingredients (except the garnish) into a long glass over ice, and stir well. Strain into a chilled cocktail glass. Garnish with fresh lime.

Preparation time: 5 minutes | Serves 1

LUNCH ALL WRAPPED UP!

HOME OF THE WORLD FAMOUS YORKYPUD™ WRAP, THE YORK ROAST CO IS A HUGELY SUCCESSFUL FAMILY-RUN BUSINESS WITH ALL THE TRIMMINGS…

Originally known as York Hog Roast, the renowned purveyor of roast meat sandwiches and a very special wrap started life as a small venture with managing director Wayne Chadwick as the sole trader. He took over a butcher's shop which had roast meats displayed in the window, and began to sell his own pork, beef, ham and turkey sandwiches in 2004. Word spread and Wayne was able to open a second shop on Stonegate just five years later, then as the company's popularity continued to climb he decided it was time to rebrand as The York Roast Co.

Having been established under the new name in Chester, the flagship shop on Stonegate opened in 2013, and the original moved next door to bigger premises. Customers continued to come back for the roast meat sandwiches – complete with stuffing, a choice of sauce and crispy crackling – but Wayne had no idea how much his next idea would transform the business. The York Roast Co's invention of the YorkyPud™ Wrap went viral after a post on social media, which gathered millions of views and led to national media attention. There's even a rap about the wrap on YouTube!

Wayne has since served his creation on BBC's The One Show, been live on air for ITV's This Morning and welcomed people from the length and breadth of the country to try the famous wrap. Who doesn't like a Sunday dinner with all the trimmings, enveloped in a giant Yorkshire pudding that you can enjoy anywhere? He also frequently gets emails from fans in Australia, Canada and other far flung places asking when The York Roast Co. will open a branch near them! Wayne and his son Stephen do have plans to expand the business with more permanent locations across the UK, joining the York, Chester and Shrewsbury shops. Two trailers currently take food on the road to weddings, festivals and other events where the same much-loved sandwiches and wraps are served.

The York Roast Co. still offers beef, pork, ham and turkey and will stick to the hand-held delights that made its name. All the pork, which is the biggest seller, is sourced within North Yorkshire and is typically topped with freshly made stuffing, a choice of sauce and crunchy crackling; no wonder it's hard for customers to resist! From humble beginnings, the company has proved its popularity time and time again and is much more than an internet craze, with top quality British ingredients and a touch of Yorkshire charm.

WAR OF THE ROSES

War of the Roses is a Lancashire hotpot encased inside a Yorkshire pudding. The recipe was created by Tom Casson, winner of The York Roast Co.'s inaugural Great Yorkshire Pudding Challenge: a national cooking competition to find the next ground-breaking Yorkshire pudding creation, held on Yorkshire Day, 1st August 2019.

FOR THE LANCASHIRE HOTPOT

1 tbsp butter

1 tbsp vegetable oil

500g lamb shoulder or neck, diced

2 brown onions, peeled and thinly sliced

1 heaped tbsp plain flour

480ml hot chicken or vegetable stock

2 bay leaves

½ tsp salt

½ tsp ground black pepper

2 tbsp Henderson's Relish

3 medium carrots, peeled and cut into 2cm chunks

680g potatoes, peeled and sliced to 2-3mm thick (Maris Pipers work best)

1 tbsp melted butter

Sprigs of fresh thyme

FOR THE YORKSHIRE PUDDINGS (MAKES 6-8)

Vegetable or sunflower oil

140g plain flour

4 eggs

200ml milk

Salt and pepper

FOR THE LANCASHIRE HOTPOT

Preheat the oven to 170°c.

Melt the butter and vegetable oil in a medium saucepan and then fry the lamb until lightly browned all over. This should take about 3 to 4 minutes. Spoon the lamb into a bowl and put the fat from the pan to one side as this will be used for the Yorkshire puddings.

Add the onions to the pan and cook for 3 to 4 minutes, stirring regularly, until soft. Put the lamb back in, then stir in the flour and cook for 1 minute. Add the stock, bay leaves, salt, pepper and Henderson's Relish to the pan. Give everything a stir and bring to a gentle simmer.

Transfer the mixture to a casserole or pie dish. Place the lid on top or cover with foil and cook in the oven for 30 minutes.

Meanwhile, par boil the carrots and potatoes for 3 to 5 minutes on a medium to high heat. Take the hotpot out of the oven, stir in the carrots and top with the sliced potatoes. Start with the outer edge and layer the potatoes to cover the top entirely, finishing in the centre.

Brush the top of the potatoes with the melted butter and sprinkle on some thyme leaves. Cover with a lid or foil and place back in the oven for 45 minutes.

After 45 minutes, turn the oven up to 200°c and remove the lid or foil. Cook for a further 45 minutes until the potatoes are browned and crisp on top. Take the hotpot out of the oven, and leave to rest for 5 minutes or so.

FOR THE YORKSHIRE PUDDINGS

Preheat the oven to 230°c. Drizzle a little oil and lamb fat evenly into each well in a 4-hole Yorkshire pudding tin or a 12-hole non-stick muffin tin and place in the oven to heat through.

To make the batter, tip the plain flour into a bowl and beat in the eggs until smooth. Gradually add the milk and continue beating until the mix is completely lump-free. Season with salt and pepper then pour the batter into a jug.

Remove the hot tins from the oven then carefully and evenly pour the batter into the wells. Place the tin straight back into the oven and leave undisturbed for 20 to 25 minutes until the puddings have risen and browned.

Serve immediately, filled with a generous helping of Lancashire hotpot.

Preparation time: 10 minutes | Cooking time: 2 hours 15 minutes | Serves: 5-6

DIRECTORY

ASHLEY MCCARTHY CHOCOLATE

Website: ashleymccarthy.co.uk
Email: chefash30@icloud.com
Telephone: 07772311873
Facebook: Ashley McCarthy Extreme Chocolate
Twitter: @AshleyMcChef
Instagram: ashleymcchef

Award-winning self-taught chocolatier, working on stunning handmade chocolates and sweet gifts as well as unique bespoke chocolate sculptures for all types of celebrations and business promotions.

BEADLAM GRANGE FARM SHOP

Beadam Grange Farm
Pockley
Nr Helmsley YO62 7TD
Telephone: 01439 770 303
Website: www.beadlamgrange.co.uk

Farm shop and tearoom with a butchery specialising in their home-bred Limousin beef.

THE BISHY WEIGH

1 Bishopthorpe Road
York
YO23 1NA
Email: hello@thebishyweigh.co.uk
Website: www.thebishyweigh.co.uk

Friendly local eco pantry on York's beautiful Bishopthorpe Road high street, offering hundreds of ingredients, toiletries and household products without plastic or packaging.

CRUMBS CUPCAKERY

10 College Street
York
YO1 7JF
Telephone: 01904 638282
Website: www.crumbs-cupcakery.co.uk

Bakery, shop and café serving freshly made cupcakes alongside afternoon and cream teas, hot drinks and other sweet treats.

EAT ME CAFE & SOCIAL

1-2 Hanover Road
Scarborough
North Yorkshire
YO11 1LS
Telephone: 07445475328
Website: www.eatmecafe.com
Facebook: Eat.Me.Cafe
Twitter & Instagram: @eatmecafe
YouTube: youtube.com/c/EatMeCafeSocial

An eclectic mix of British and Asian food with speciality coffee and all-day cocktails, served in a quirky and sociable atmosphere.

EVIL EYE

42 Stonegate
York YO1 8AS
Telephone: 01904 640 002
Website: www.evileyelounge.com

The best cocktail bar in the North, with over 120 cocktails on our menu made with fresh ingredients, also housing our Guinness World Record-holding gin shop.

THE CAFÉ AT FIELD AND FAWCETT

Field and Fawcett Wine Merchants
The Old Dairy
Bingley House Farm
Grimston Bar
York YO19 5LA
Telephone: 01904 489073
Email: info@fieldandfawcett.co.uk
Website: www.fieldandfawcett.co.uk

Family-owned and run wine merchants, deli and café. Passionate about quality and providing the best from breakfast and lunch to homemade cakes.

THE GRANTLEY BAR AND RESTAURANT

High Grantley
Near Ripon HG4 3PJ
Telephone: 01765 620 227
Website: www.grantleyarms.com

Fine dining in a picturesque 17th-century inn, set between Ripon and Harrogate.

GRANTLEY HALL

Ripon
North Yorkshire
HG4 3ET
Telephone: 01765 620 070
Website: www.grantleyhall.co.uk

Luxury five star hotel and wellness retreat located on the edge of the Yorkshire Dales, which offers 47 exquisite rooms and suites, four diverse dining options and extensive leisure facilities.

HAXBY BAKEHOUSE

The Village
Haxby
York YO32 3SA
Tel: 01904 765 878
Website: www.haxbybakehouse.co.uk

York's artisan bakery and delicatessen, specialising in award-winning sourdough.

JERVAULX ABBEY TEAROOM

Jervaulx
Ripon HG4 4PH
Telephone: 01677 460 391
Website: www.jervaulxabbey.com

Specialising in delicious homemade cakes and baked goods, as well as freshly cooked light meals made with Yorkshire produce by the family who own and maintain the spectacular Jervaulx Abbey.

LOVE CHEESE

16 Gillygate
York YO31 7EQ
Telephone: 01904 622 967
Website: www.lovecheese.co.uk

York's only specialist cheese shop, café and online shop.

NORTHERN FOX YORKSHIRE GIN

41 Valley Drive
Kirk Ella HU10 7PW
Telephone: 07943 066 192
Website: www.foxgins.co.uk

Small-volume, handmade artisan gin from Yorkshire, with an ethos of whenever possible using Yorkshire flavours, producers, suppliers and retailers.

THE PIEBALD INN

65 Sands Lane
Hunmanby
Filey
YO14 0LT
Telephone: 01723 447577
Website: www.thepiebaldinn.co.uk

Destination pub with a menu of over 50 proper pies from the traditional to the adventurous, a collection of over 100 gins plus cask ales and wines, seven luxury bedrooms and a large sun terrace.

THE PLOUGH INN

21–23 High Street
Scalby
North Yorkshire
YO13 0PT
Telephone: 01723 362622
Website: www.theploughscalby.co.uk

Village pub, restaurant and luxury accommodation with a focus on food made with peak quality local produce, alongside spectacular cocktails and Yorkshire ales.

ROOTS YORK

68 Marygate
York
YO30 7BH
Email: info@rootsyork.co.uk
Website: www.rootsyork.com

Restaurant by the Banks family of The Black Swan at Oldstead, serving small plates and a feast menu steeped in their unique approach to seasonality and made with home-grown produce all year round.

SKOSH

98 Micklegate
York YO1 6JX
Telephone: 01904 634 849
Website: www.skoshyork.co.uk
Contemporary British cooking with an international influence. Snacks and small plates.

THE SPIRIT OF YORKSHIRE DISTILLERY

The Distillery
Hunmanby Industrial Estate
Hunmanby YO14 0PH
Telephone: 01723 891758
Website: www.spiritofyorkshire.com
Yorkshire's first whisky distillery, making field to bottle whisky. Home of Filey Bay Single Malt and the Pot Still Coffee Shop, a coffee roaster and tea merchant where you can watch your coffee being roasted and enjoy a brew in a Victorian coffee house.

VALE OF MOWBRAY

20 Leases Road
Leeming Bar
Northallerton DL7 9AW
Telephone: 01677 422661
Website: www.valeofmowbray.co.uk
Proud Yorkshire-based pork pie producers, making pies right since 1928.

VISIT YORK

1 Museum Street
York
North Yorkshire YO1 7DT
Telephone: 01904 555670
Website: www.visityork.org
Visit York markets York as a must-see world-class destination to the leisure visitor. The organisation ensures investment develops the quality of tourism in the city and provides a visitor information service.

WENSLEYDALE CREAMERY

Gayle Lane
Hawes, Wensleydale
North Yorkshire DL8 3RN
Telephone: 01969 667 664
Website: www.wensleydale.co.uk
The Wensleydale Creamery, based at Hawes in Wensleydale in the heart of the Yorkshire Dales National Park, is home of the famous Yorkshire Wensleydale cheese and a popular Visitor Centre.

WHERE THE RIBBON ENDS

at Jervaulx Abbey Tearoom
Jervaulx
Ripon HG4 4PH
Email: wheretheribbonends@gmail.com
Website: www.wheretheribbonends.com
Specialising in creating beautiful and elegant wedding cakes which are individually made with passion, care and the utmost attention to detail.

THE WHIPPET INN

15 North Street
York YO1 6JD
Telephone: 01904 500 660
Website: www.thewhippetinn.co.uk
Lovingly referred to as 'York's hidden gem', this independent restaurant has garnered a reputation for using amazing local produce to create delicious plates of food.

THE WHOLE HOGG FARM SHOP AND TEAROOM.

Howebridge Farm
Low Marishes
Malton YO17 6RQ
Telephone: 01653 669 469
Website: www.thewholehoggfarmshop.co.uk
Family-run farm shop and tea room on a traditional working farm.

YORK GIN SHOP

12 Pavement
York YO1 9UP
Telephone: 07860 920 298

YORK GIN DISTILLERY & DISTILLERY SHOP

Unit 1, Acaster Estate
Cowper Lane
York YO23 2TX
Telephone: 01904 848 900
Website: www.yorkgin.com
Award-winning gin, handmade in the city of York.

THE YORK ROAST CO.

78 Low Petergate
York YO1 7HZ
Telephone: 01904 629197
Website: theyorkroastco.com
With a passion for high quality British ingredients served with a touch of Yorkshire charm, The York Roast Co. offers hearty hand-carved meat sandwiches and the world-famous YorkyPud™ Wrap.

OTHER TITLES AVAILABLE

The Little Book of Cakes & Bakes

Featuring recipes and stories from the kitchens of some of the nation's best bakers and cake-makers.
9781910863480

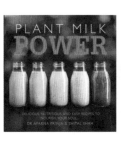

Plant Milk Power

How to create your own delicious, nutritious and nourishing moo-free milks and smoothies.
9781910863411

Tasty & Healthy

Eating well with lactose intolerance, coeliac disease, Crohn's disease, ulcerative colitis and irritable bowel syndrome.
9781910863367

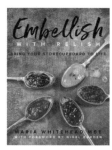

Embellish with Relish

Bring your store cupboard essentials to life with The Hawkshead Relish Cook Book. From hearty hotpots to aromatic curries, these are simple but satisfying meals packed full of flavour. 9781910863497

Sweet Chilli Friday

Simple vegetarian recipes from our kitchen to yours.
9781910863381

RECENT TITLES FROM OUR 'GET STUCK IN' SERIES

The Bristol and Bath Cook Book features Pinkmans Bakery, featured in The Sunday Times Top 25 bakeries in the UK, The Fish Shop and steak specialists Pasture.
9781910863558

Lancashire Second Helpings
Features acclaimed-Lancastrian Steve Smith from the Freemasons at Wiswell, local favourite The Cartford Inn, award-winning Cuckoo Gin and events from Visit Lancashire.
9781910863510

The Cornish Cook Book
Featuring Gylly Beach, winner of 'Best Café' in the Southwest 2018, The Rising Sun, Cornwall Life's Pub of the Year and Edie's Kitchen run by Nigel Brown.
978-1-910863-47-3

The Edinburgh and East Coast Cook Book
features Masterchef winner Jamie Scott at The Newport, Fhior, Pickering's Gin, Pie Not, Stockbridge Market and much more.
978-1-910863-45-9

The Glasgow and West Coast Cook Book
features The Gannet, Two Fat Ladies, The Spanish Butcher, Hutchesons City Grill, Gamba and much more.
978-1-910863-43-5

The Bristol Cook Book
features Dean Edwards, Lido, Clifton Sausage, The Ox, and wines from Corks of Cotham plus lots more.
978-1-910863-14-5

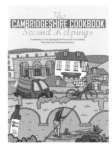

The Cambridgeshire Cook Book: Second Helpings
features Mark Abbott of Midsummer House, The Olive Grove, Elder Street Café and much more.
978-1-910863-33-6

The Manchester Cook Book: Second Helpings
features Ben Mounsey of Grafene, Hatch, Refuge, Masons, Old School BBQ Bus and much more.
978-1-910863-44-2

The Bath Cook Book
features more than 40 recipes from The Chequers, Hare & Hounds, The Beaufort and Blue Quails Deli plus much more.
9781910863176

The Derbyshire Cook Book: Second Helpings
features Chris Mapp at The Tickled Trout, Chatsworth Farm Shop, Michelin-starred Fischer's, Peacock and much more.
978-1-910863-34-3

All our books are available from Waterstones, Amazon and good independent bookshops.
FIND OUT MORE ABOUT US AT WWW.MEZEPUBLISHING.CO.UK